Melanin Magic

A YOUNG MYSTIC'S GUIDE TO AFRICAN SPIRITUALITY

DOSSÉ-VIA TRENOU
Illustrated by Catmouse James

RP|KIDS
PHILADELPHIA

This book is dedicated to Nova, Rémy,
and young mystics of all ages.

Running Press Kids
Hachette Book Group
1290 Avenue of the Americas, New York, NY 10104
www.runningpress.com/rpkids
@runningpresskids

Distributed in the United Kingdom by Little, Brown Book Group UK,
Carmelite House, 50 Victoria Embankment, London, EC4Y 0DZ

First Edition: October 2024

Published by Running Press Kids, an imprint of Hachette Book Group, Inc.
The Running Press Kids name and logo are trademarks
of Hachette Book Group, Inc.

The Hachette Speakers Bureau provides a wide range of authors
for speaking events. To find out more, go to www.hachettespeakersbureau.com
or email HachetteSpeakers@hbgusa.com.

Running Press books may be purchased in bulk for business, educational,
or promotional use. For more information, please contact your local bookseller
or the Hachette Book Group Special Markets Department at
Special.Markets@hbgusa.com.

The publisher is not responsible for websites (or their content)
that are not owned by the publisher.

Print book cover and interior design by Frances J. Soo Ping Chow

Library of Congress Control Number: 2023036921

ISBNs: 978-0-7624-8448-5 (hardcover), 978-0-7624-8449-2 (ebook)

Printed in Guangdong, China

1010

10 9 8 7 6 5 4 3 2 1

CONTENTS

AUTHOR'S NOTE

What if I told you the magic you've been looking for already exists within yourself?

My name is Dossé-Via Trenou, and I am a daughter of the continent now known as Africa. In many African communities, cultural tales and beliefs are passed down orally through storytelling. In this book, I invite you into a special wonderland. You'll learn about Africa's magic and wisdom through the world of two fictional characters (meaning I made up their existence with my imagination) attending Forest Magic School: Yawa and Kossi.

Yawa and Kossi are the middle names of my actual children, Nova and Rémy, and this book is inspired by the adventures we have together while living on the African continent, as well as the lessons we've learned and continue to learn each day. It is my dream that every child interested in their melanin magic will be able to visit the countries of Africa and feel at home there.

To the young mystic reading this, keep in mind that while Yawa's and Kossi's adventures at Forest Magic School exist as a figment of our imagination, the teachings in the mystical forest, including what the forest scholars learn in their classes, can be applied to your life, no matter where you are. You're reading this for a reason. You're a scholar at Forest Magic School, too. Whether you live near a forest or are thinking about a forest in your mind, you're also learning the teachings and the teachings are learning you. So travel along, forest friend. You can teleport with the power of your mind. You can create the future. You can revisit the past. And you can embrace the present. Your ancestors knew and did this, and you can too.

Melanin Magic is an invitation for you to travel to a spiritual world and be part of it in your own unique way. If you don't yet know what African spirituality is, my intention is that by the end of this book you'll feel more familiar with it. Enjoy the journey!

Ready? Let's go.

The Magic Portal

Yawa and Kossi had a feeling that by the time they returned from their grandparents' home in the forest, they'd view their lives with a new set of eyes.

The siblings had been dreaming of this day for as long as they could remember, and now they were entering the portal.

The ancestral portal, their parents loved to call it.

Their parents were quite excited about Kossi's and Yawa's birthdays, which had taken place the day before. Yawa and Kossi were both born on the same day—June 6—but two years apart. For this reason, combined with their striking similarities, their friends and family nicknamed Yawa and Kossi the "almost-twins."

Yawa had just turned eleven, and Kossi was now nine. Their mother often reminded them that their birthday, or **solar return**, symbolized a **rite of passage** and that no one was better to usher them into their **solar new year** than their grandparents.

Yawa and Kossi were off to Forest Magic School in the village of Bambo, in the heart of the Ivorian forest on the western side of the African continent. That's where Mami and Papi lived, and that's where Yawa and Kossi were going to explore over the next nine weeks.

And through reading this African spirituality guide, you, too, can join them at Forest Magic School.

Forest Magic School is a mystical summer school where people from all over the African continent, and the diaspora, come to learn about their roots. Diaspora refers to the spread of people away from their native homeland. In this case, many forest scholars have ancestors who once lived in Africa and who left the continent by force or by choice. Now the forest scholars were returning. And in a way, their ancestors were returning, too.

The children and preteens who made their way to Forest Magic School each summer came from different regions of the world. They were called forest scholars, and they attended the school to explore the universe of the West African forest and to learn about African spirituality. And they were also here to make some forest friends!

"Kossi, what should we do first?" Yawa asked her brother as they parked their bikes beneath their grandparents' welcoming tree house. Yawa and Kossi admired their surroundings. Their grandparents' home felt so grounded in nature and free. They could hear drums beating in the distance. They loved seeing the earth's red soil, and they felt safe being surrounded by greenery. They admired the butterflies that fluttered by and the playful monkeys that spontaneously greeted them from the trees' branches.

"We should leave an offering to the ancestors," Kossi calmly responded. "To thank them for bringing us here and to let them know we'll need their help and guidance on this journey."

"Absolutely," Yawa replied as she pulled out mangoes and water from her backpack.

An offering is a symbolic or physical present that we give to our spirit guides or ancestors.

As she poured water onto the rust-colored soil, Yawa heard a familiar voice coming from their grandparents' backyard: "Are these my magically melanated mystics who've just arrived?"

"Yes, it's us!" Kossi and Yawa replied in unison to Mami. Then, as if by magic, Papi appeared from behind the garden's rosebush, holding a tray of glasses filled with **bissap** and ginger juice.

"Woézon!" Papi said. Woézon means *welcome* in the Ewe (pronounced *Eh-veh*) language of Togo, which is where Papi and Mami spent most of their lives before moving to the Bambo Forest.

Everyone's eyes filled with tears of joy. They ran to one another and fell into a warm embrace. The mango tree's leaves quietly provided them with shade—and it even seemed to smile back at them.

And so the adventure began.

After dinner, the almost-twins and their grandparents looked at family photos on the wall of the cabin house. Papi had built the house by hand with the help of the village thirty-five years ago. In the Bambo Forest, and in many West African communities, people rarely did things alone. The village was always there to help. One big community and ecosystem. Just like the forest.

Mami and Papi had lovingly created a book that contained a family tree made from images. This was a way to honor the Tree of Life, which represents lineage—a group of humans connected to a common ancestor. Trees within trees of Kossi and Yawa's family history were displayed like a living altar.

> An altar is a table or special area used to worship,
> protect, or honor something or someone.

Looking at these images connected Kossi and Yawa to their ancestors, elders, and memories. There were also framed images of the almost-twins from their birth up until their birthdays last year. This helped track their evolution as human beings, as well as their growth.

Mami and Papi had placed a special table in each of the almost-twins' rooms where they could create an altar of their own, either for living family members, for those who had died, or for both.

Have you ever created an altar before, Forest Scholar?

How to Create an Altar

- **Decide what or whom you'd like to honor or celebrate.** Our ancestors are family members (either your biological family or people you feel a strong connection to) who are no longer physically with us but who are present with us spiritually. If you have specific ancestors with whom you feel a strong connection, or those you want to deepen your connection to, you may want to make a special place for them on your altar. You can also create living altars where you honor your current blood or soul family, such as your parents, siblings, grandparents, cousins, pets, and your own selves.
- **Choose a table and an area of your home or room where you'd like the altar to be.** Ideally this would be a spot that doesn't have too much activity around it, because altars are about purifying and protecting energy, with the help of your spirit guide. Purify your chosen space through lighting incense around the altar (ask a trusted adult for help whenever you use matches or items with flames). You can put a white tablecloth on the altar, or if you prefer, you can choose

a **kente cloth** for the table (like what Kossi and Yawa did with their altars). Your altar should make you feel joyful when you look at it and when you're near it, so take your time deciding its location and giving it the vibe you want.

- **Choose mementos or special objects that help you feel connected with whatever or whomever you chose to honor on your altar.** This could be displaying a portrait of that person, their favorite perfume, their favorite accessory, or whatever feels right to you. Yawa placed a portrait of her great-great-grandmother Vovo on her altar because her mother often told her that they had similar temperaments and that they looked alike.
- Make sure the elements of **air**, **water**, **fire**, **earth**, and/or **minerals** are present on the altar in some way. This could be the following:
  - Air element: Adding a feather, which can represent the air.
  - Water element: Setting a fresh glass of water on your altar, ideally in a cup you can see through. Change the water regularly, at least once a week.
  - Fire element: Lighting a candle, with a parent or guardian's help, or adding decorative string lights to your altar.
  - Earth element: Placing your favorite stone or protective crystal on the altar.
  - Minerals element: Adding some sand from your favorite beach to the altar.

Yawa and Kossi loved creating their altars with some of the special items they had brought with them in their summer schoolbags. The almost-twins went to sleep that night surrounded by the protective energy of their parents and ancestors, who were watching and praying over them.

At breakfast the next morning, Mami and Papi answered Yawa's and Kossi's questions about what to expect at Forest Magic School.

"Will we like our teachers?" Kossi asked as he drank his tapioca broth.

Tapioca is a form of cassava, made from its starch.
When made as a breakfast broth, it has a pudding-like
texture and slightly bitter taste. Honey, lemon,
and fruit such as blueberries can be yummy additions.

"I think the trees will be our teachers!" Yawa excitedly shared. "Maybe that's why it's called Forest Magic School." She broke off a piece of sweet bread and added some honey to it.

"Forest Magic School's been around for a while," Papi said as he poured more tapioca broth into Kossi's and Yawa's mugs made of natural clay. "The trees are absolutely here to teach us, Yawa. And you'll soon see there are *many* reasons we call this Forest Magic School."

"I'm like a tree," Yawa responded as she stretched her arms upward toward the sky. "Still growing."

"That you are. Let's go for a walking tour of the village after breakfast," Papi suggested. "I'm sure you'll find plenty of tree friends to grow with."

Yawa and Kossi had been to the village before. They visited their grandparents each summer. The forest always felt like a safe space to them, even with all the wild animals that lived among them. They never knew when they'd run into a group of chimpanzees crossing their path or see a snake slithering or bats flying across the night skies. They always knew there was a tree nearby for them to hug, talk to, or play with. They were familiar with the forest and its wonder, but there was more to explore. And this was the first summer they were attending Forest Magic School.

As they left the cabin house, Papi reminded them that their nine-week adventure was an introduction to the world of African spirituality, which is all about learning and respecting the magic of Africa. They were ready to see what the magic was about.

"The magic is all around you," Papi calmly explained as they made their way down a long, winding path leading to the center of the village. "Most of life's magic can be found in the simple things. Especially what we tend to take for granted. Look around you, almost-twins. What do you see?"

Kossi ran ahead of Yawa and Papi and observed the medicine woman collecting herbs from the community garden. Yawa played in the large puddles of water resting in the middle of her path. She remembered it was the rainy season. Papi paused as he noticed four ant trails being formed before his eyes. The almost-twins ran to his side and watched as the ants moved about busily, each performing their role in the larger community mission. As the family made their way to their favorite river, in the center of the forest, Yawa and Kossi said hi to the tatas and tontons (Ivorian words for "aunties" and "uncles" who may not actually be related to your family but still feel like family) hanging their clothes to dry on a clothesline. Kossi was pleasantly distracted by the smell of yam chips being fried by the tata with the beautifully cornrowed hair, who was carrying her daughter on her back. To get to Forest Magic School, they had to cross a bridge over the river, then wait patiently for the school to appear from behind a seemingly endless amount of banana trees and their leaves, which swayed in the wind. But the Forest Magic School building only appeared when classes were in session. The almost-twins had to wait a bit longer.

"This is the path you'll take each day to get to Forest Magic School. You're just one night away from entering the ancestral portal," Papi said as he smiled at his grandchildren. "Are you ready?"

"We're ready!" Yawa and Kossi exclaimed.

What about you, Forest Scholar? Are you ready, too?

CHAPTER 1

Your Ori and Your Breath

On the first day of Forest Magic School, the almost-twins arrived in their classroom, named the Bamboo Room because most of the materials in the room—the walls, the chairs, and the tables—were made of bamboo. The almost-twins saw a human wearing all white, from their white turban to white sandals. The human was calmly looking out the window and observing the trees blowing in the wind. There were eight children in the class, including the almost-twins. As the forest scholars came in one by one, they all sat in a circle and observed the pensive human.

Once everyone had arrived, the human turned around, took a deep breath in and out, smiled at the scholars, and said, "Akwaaba!" which means *welcome* in Baoulé, one of the languages of Côte d'Ivoire. Many other African languages—such as Twi (from the country of Ghana), Ewe (from the region of Togo), Fon (from the Republic of Bénin), Swahili (the most common language in Africa, spoken in countries such as Kenya, Tanzania, South Sudan, Rwanda, and more), Lingala (Congo), and Wolof (Sénégal)—were spoken at Forest Magic School. Scholars also spoke English, French, Spanish, Portuguese, Mandarin, and countless other languages.

The forest scholars in all the classrooms were young mystics. They had traveled from all over the world to learn at this magical summer school because they had heard about the transformative—meaning a force that creates a huge change—powers of African spirituality. An essential part of African spirituality has to do with *being present with yourself and honoring your roots, your ancestors, nature, and the energies of the cosmos*. It has transformative powers because it helps you remember truths about yourself that you might have otherwise forgotten. Since much of modern society tends to be disconnected from nature, and nature is at the core of African spirituality, being connected to nature helps awaken young mystics' spirits. When used with care, African spirituality helps you remember yourself and your purpose for being on earth.

"I'm Professor Ori," the human dressed all in white said calmly. The professor sat in the circle among the curious children. Kossi and Yawa sat across from each other, and their eyes widened with wonder at what this school experience would be like. "What are your names?"

One by one, Akua, Sundiata, Ife, Michael, Kossi, Yawa, Clémentine, and Felipe introduced themselves and shared where they were from. The almost-twins, Ife, Sundiata, and Akua lived in the West African countries of Côte d'Ivoire, Ghana, and Nigeria. Michael came from the Dominican Republic, an island in the Caribbean. Clémentine was born in France, but her parents were from the East African country of Kenya. And Felipe lived primarily in Harlem, New York, but he viewed himself as a citizen of the world.

Professor Ori gave each forest scholar a thick journal made of papyrus—the original paper from Ancient Egypt. The region of Africa known as Ancient Egypt was previously called Kemet, and it was a world filled with magically melanated beings. *(You'll learn more about melanin and its magic soon, as will the young mystics in the Bamboo Room.)* Each papyrus journal was broken into nine chapters, to represent the nine weeks of Forest Magic School. Professor Ori instructed the scholars to write their insights from each week in their journal. They could choose what notes felt most important to them and write them down. *(For the young mystic reading this, if you have a special journal, use it to write down your forest learnings. There's a lot to learn!)*

Scholars also each received their own SpacePad. SpacePads are eco-friendly devices that connect the scholars to the digital world—in moderation. Moderation means finding a sense of balance and not taking things to extremes. It's an important concept in African spirituality. *(Even what you're learning here should be taken in moderately, and you should trust your own instincts when it comes to what it means to be spiritual.)*

"Being present with nature is a great way to activate your *melanin magic*," Professor Ori told the scholars as they logged in to their SpacePads. "Let's be mindful of how much technology we consume. When taken to extremes, technology can suffocate our spirits."

The scholars could use their SpacePads to do research, take notes, and write their own stories. There was a time limit to how long they could use the SpacePads, and they never knew when the device would turn off. This was how the SpacePad made it possible to let the forest scholars' brains rest. That's why they were called SpacePads—they gave their brains, and their Oris, space to figure things out on their own, using *internal* intelligence.

"It's time for you to learn a bit more about what it means to be a forest scholar. At Forest Magic School, forest scholars are encouraged to explore, to experiment, to dream, to question, to study, and to reimagine," said Professor Ori.

The professor explained how forest scholars learn through a variety of paths, using their intuition to guide them, like a compass. The forest scholars are also teachers. The professors learn just as much from the scholars as the scholars learn from the professors. This is called **intergenerational learning**.

"Beyond these bamboo walls, we view the universe around us as our school and living laboratory," Professor Ori shared, with twinkles of passion sparkling in their eyes.

The Bamboo Room scholars soon learned that at Forest Magic School, scholars aren't given a typical report card at the end of the semester. Instead, they're encouraged to view their papyrus journals as *road maps to remembrance*, helping them to think back and ponder their roots, their ancestry, and their personal stories.

"If there's one thing to keep in mind during your time at Forest Magic School," said Professor Ori, "it's that *the forest helps you remember who you are and who you can become*. Akpé kaka means *thank you very much* in Mina, one of Togo's many languages. Akpé kaka for being here, young learners."

Forest Scholar reading this book: Get out your favorite journal, because you're also on this journey as a young mystic. Akwaaba, and akpé kaka for being here.

"Do you know what your **Ori** is?" the professor asked when the scholars reunited in the learning circle after lunch. They had eaten boiled yam with black-eyed peas and green beans, accompanied by fresh coconut water to stay hydrated.

At first, the class was silent, and the scholars seemed somewhat shy. Everyone looked around to see who'd be the first to answer.

Yawa remembered her mother often telling her about the magic of trusting and honoring one's Ori. It was one of the first reflections she had written in her journal as a younger child. When she remembered what her mother had shared with her about the Ori's wisdom, she smiled and understood why Professor Ori had brought it up.

After a few seconds of reflection, Yawa said, "Our Ori is our divine head. Our intuition. Our inner powers reflected within us. Our Ori helps us better know and love ourselves."

The professor took a deep breath and clapped their hands in appreciation of Yawa's response. "Yes, indeed, wise one."

Professor Ori continued, "I come from the region of West Africa that used to be called Yorùbáland. In Yorùbá spirituality, our Ori is our inner guidance. It literally means 'the head.' Being guided by our Ori is a powerful way to live a life aligned with your spirit. The forest is here to help you tap into the power of *your* Ori, by trusting yourself and your body. By week nine of Forest Magic School, your Ori will probably tingle as you celebrate your graduation."

The professor smiled at the scholars as if they were peering into the future and already seeing that moment happen.

"Open up your forest journals, scholars," said Professor Ori, "and write a letter to your divine head. Tell yourself what you'd like to experience, learn, remember, and teach these next nine weeks. Dream as much as you'd like to dream. That's your only assignment for today—connect with Ori."

Akua, the student next to Kossi, seemed to be the youngest of the group. She had carefully listened to what Yawa and the professor had said, and yet she seemed to still be a bit confused.

"How do I connect with my Ori?" Akua asked quietly.

"Akua, your Ori is connected to your breath. That, too, is a form of divine knowing, young mystics."

Kossi and Yawa thought they knew how to breathe, but they soon realized that perhaps they didn't know all there was to it.

What about you? Do you know the importance of breathing properly?

Professor Ori encouraged the young learners to do clockwork breathwork. This was when they took a few minutes to consciously breathe. Each day they'd add an additional minute to the meditation. The first day they did this exercise, the class moved around restlessly, especially those who hadn't practiced meditation before. Instead of shaming them, Professor Ori encouraged them. "Trying, and getting started, is often the most challenging part, forest friends."

Breathing Techniques
for Young Mystics

- **Flower Breaths:** Imagine you are smelling your favorite flower or food. Take a deep breath to inhale the scent. Close your eyes if it feels good to do so. Then slowly let the breath out through your mouth, as if the scent is being spread through your mouth out into the universe. Take your time as you release the breath. Repeat as needed. Imagine different flowers that smell *so* good you can't help but want to take more deep breaths.
- **Belly Breaths:** Feel your breath all the way in your belly by taking such a deep inhalation that your stomach seems to fill with air. Place one hand on your heart and one hand on your belly. Pay attention to the way your belly fills up when you take a breath in and then deflates when you slowly release the breath.

To integrate the Ori (your divine head) into your breathing exercises, repeat the technique of your choice above, but start rotating your head in circles in a clocklike motion. First bend your head toward the left, then put your neck up toward the sky, and then slowly turn your head to the right near your right ear. Then drop your head down and go around in a circle again. Once you've done this five times in a row, switch directions and go from right to left, slow and steady. This will help align your breath with your Ori.

And voilà! You're doing clockwork breathwork.

How to Tap into the Power of Your Ori

- Spend more time in nature than you do on digital devices.
- When you use digital devices, be mindful of what you consume. Pay attention to how your body feels when you consume it, and stop immediately if your body feels uncomfortable.
- Be aware of what you physically put into your body. The more fruits and vegetables and wholesome meals you eat, the better your Ori feels.
- Keep a clean environment, as much as you're able to, even if it starts off with tidying up your bedroom.
- Ask for help, or admit when you don't know something.
- Pour water on your head—it immediately activates your Ori. A morning shower is a great way to get your Ori going.
- Sing to yourself like you'd sing to a plant. If you give your caregivers permission, they can sing to you when you are asleep and let you know what they love about you. (Kossi and Yawa's parents often share praises of gratitude and bliss

for their children. *"Thank you for choosing us as your parents."* The almost-twins' Oris would hear these affirmations in their sleep.)

- Tell your Ori loving affirmations such as *I'm grateful for being alive. Dear Ori, help me live a spiritually aligned life today, and every day.* Do this each day when you wake up, and share that energy in the world throughout the day. Also pray to your Ori before going to sleep at night.

- One more way to tap into your Ori: *Always remember the power of the breath.* Just like the wind that blows through the forest and gifts us with purified air, your own body deserves to consistently have access to your breath and to more life.

As Yawa walked out of the Bamboo Room after having written her Ori a letter, she saw a field of lilies, and she looked up at the skies. Yawa felt inspired and activated. An orange butterfly landed on her right shoulder.

It's a good omen, Yawa thought to herself.

> An omen is a sign from the universe, often shown through symbolism, which refers to using symbols, designs, or motifs to share a message or idea.

Yawa's *third eye* was blessed by the sun's rays, and she felt amazing.

Your third eye is also known as your *pineal gland*, and it represents your intuitive knowing and your emotional sensitivity to life. The pineal gland is between your eyes, in the center of your forehead, but it's not necessarily visible (it exists beneath the layers of your skin, in a more cosmic sense). Everyone has a third eye, but not all third eyes have been fully opened. The Kemites (Ancient Egyptians, as you learned about earlier) drew illustrations of their third eye in pyramid temples. Being in touch with your inner knowing takes *patience and presence*.

Cosmic Considerations

DMT is in your third eye. DMT is the chemical that's released when a person dies, or "transitions" as some prefer to say. It's known as "the spirit molecule." Every time you raise your head near the sun and allow its rays to bless your forehead, you're stimulating your third eye and activating the spirit molecule. This connects you even more deeply to your Ori. You're activating your *melanin magic*.

You're invited to tap into your third-eye energy and to remember that the source of knowledge exists within you already. There's no need to constantly seek external sources. Tune in to yourself first. Very much like your Ori, both are connected to each other.

The scholars were given a homework assignment, or rather *Growth Work*, as Professor Ori called it. On their papyrus journals, they wrote down their Growth Work of the day, *which can also be your Growth Work, too, since you're part of Forest Magic School:*

If you could draw/create a trail that leads you to wherever you'd like to be, or wherever you dream of being, what would you draw? Visualize that trail frequently in your third eye, and picture yourself from a bird's-eye view, walking along that trail daily, discovering new wonders, people, and experiences along

the way, all while knowing that it's leading you to your dream destination—or to something even better.

Remember that you already are at that dream destination simply by being on the path that you've envisioned in your mind. You already are your dream destination. This already is your dream life. Be present and patient. It will make sense soon if it doesn't already.

Growth Work

Forest Scholar, join the Bamboo class and open up your journal to a blank page. Have fun visualizing and drawing a trail to your dream destination(s).

CHAPTER 2

Time Travel

The second week of Forest Magic School focused on traveling through time. For one hour, scholars could enter the Tree Capsule Portal as a class, and that hour would feel like an entire day to them. They could teleport to anywhere on the African continent and diaspora (the past, present, or future) and come back to tell about it. In African spirituality, most history is shared orally (from mouth to ear) rather than written. Forest Magic School's "Travel, Show, and Tell" class for young mystics was a way to keep that oral transmission, and tradition, going.

The scholars rotated who chose a new time-travel adventure to go on. Today, Michael's name was drawn from the traveling hat, and he chose to travel through time to the Caribbean, where he was from.

The Tree Capsule Portal took the forest scholars to the Dominican Republic, a country in the Caribbean that borders Haiti. Both Haiti and the DR have large populations of people who previously lived in Africa before being taken by force during the enslavement trade. The enslavement trade took place from around 1501 to 1867. Tens of millions of Africans were forced onto ships and sent to North and South America, and the Caribbean, to work as enslaved humans. The majority of those enslaved never returned to the African continent—physically, at least. Spiritually—that's a different story. And luckily for us, some of their descendants did make it back, just like Michael and his family.

"Meet my brother, Adam," Michael said, once the scholars had adjusted to their new location, which was on a stunning beach with a palm tree–lined shore. "We call him Ascension Adam because he likes to meditate. He views meditation as a way to fly high above life's stress and just be chill."

Adam was only fourteen years old, but he was already an expert at yoga and meditation. Ascension Adam leads a yoga class each day at sunset on the beach, and it is open to forest friends of all ages. A martial artist by nature, Ascension Adam also practices capoeira, boxing, and jiujitsu.

"I do taekwondo," Yawa proudly exclaimed as they joined Ascension Adam under his favorite palm tree. "When did you start training?"

Ascension Adam suddenly did a roundhouse kick above Yawa's head as she launched into the starter position, prepared for his next move. "I started to train in jiujitsu because I lived in a big city with a lot of dangerous people who could harm you. I wanted to feel confident in myself, and martial artists seemed to have that. I then started yoga to make my body feel better, as my limbs ached. *When you listen to your body, your body listens to you.*"

Ascension Adam took a deep breath, poured some water onto his Ori, and instructed the class to enter *Child's pose*, to transition into a new dimension, with the power of their breath and presence. Just as the class was getting into a calm vibration with their knees bent and spread apart, and their arms outstretched in front of them, they heard drumming in the distance growing closer to their meditation spot. The drums were getting louder and louder.

"Should we go somewhere with less noise?" Felipe wondered aloud.

"Let's try to create that sense of quiet right here, right now, even amid the sound of the drums. You can find stillness and peace wherever you are, my friends. Whether it's a city, yoga class, or a boxing match . . . just breathe, take your time, center yourself."

So the forest scholars breathed. They took their time. They centered themselves.

Benefits of Meditation

- Directly connects the universe around and within you to your Ori.
- Helps manage emotions.
- Helps you pay attention to your breathing.
- Relieves stress as you release tension and anxiety.
- Develops mindfulness.
- Helps reduce addiction to technology, sugar, drama, and more.

"There are many ways to amplify your energy," Ascension Adam shared as the class sat down in the learning circle on the beach after their meditation. "Can you think of any?"

"Sleeping!" said Felipe as he yawned. That meditation session was making him feel mellow and ready for a nap.

"Drinking water!" added Clémentine.

"Eating fruits and veggies," shared Kossi.

"Great job, scholars! I can tell you're full of energy already. What else?"

"Exercising and spending time in nature!" Yawa exclaimed.

"Absolutely. Two of my favorite activities ever. I also feel a boost of energy when I journal, read, or create something like a song or poem. Or when I listen to peaceful music or set an intention under the new moon. Also, when you spend time with your pet or a friend, you amplify your energy."

"What drains our energy then?" asked Sundiata.

"Too much screen time, for sure. And even sunlight must be absorbed in moderation or else it could burn you and take away your energy through dehydration. Not drinking enough water. Eating junk food. Saying yes to people when you really want to say no. Having a messy living or working environment. Not getting enough sleep or sunlight. Unhealthy friends or family connections. Speaking badly about yourself or others. All these take away from our energy."

The scholars wrote these notes down in their papyrus journals.

Forest Scholar: Can you think of other ways that our energy is amplified or drained? When do you feel your best?

"The good news is," Ascension Adam said as he rolled out the yoga mats and officially began the session, "through yoga and meditation, you can always refill your cup. With each breath, and each stretch, you begin again. The Kemites practiced a form of yoga called *Kemetic yoga*." Ascension Adam pulled out a manual that seemed to be hundreds of years old and showed the scholars some of those ancient poses.

"Many of the Kemetic yoga poses are used today in various ways in several yoga practices. The core of Kemetic yoga is focusing on the body's movements to feel more connected to one's mind and soul. There's more of a focus on meditation and taking things slowly in Kemetic yoga. It's only once you are fully in a meditative state that you can begin physical movement. Most of the Kemetic poses you'll practice today were found in Kemetic pyramids and temples. If you ever find yourself in Egypt, scholars, go to the ancient temples in Luxor and Aswan. You'll see many of these poses drawn on the temple walls."

Below are some Kemetic yoga techniques. These can be modified if you're in a wheelchair or have a physical disability, so only do the poses that feel accessible to you.

Kemetic Yoga Techniques

- **Breathe:** always come back to this, as this is the life force. Remember the Rule of 4: inhale, pause, exhale, pause.
- **Cactus pose of Selket:** stand or sit tall, and take care of your posture. Have your own back.
- **Happy baby pose:** to do this pose, turn yourself into a ball by rolling onto your back, bending your legs, and holding each foot in each hand. This pose helps relieve stress in your back (called spine work), and it's proven to increase happiness!
- **Nefertum pose (also known as Lotus pose):** sit with your legs crossed. Place your right foot on top of your left knee, and your left foot on top of your right knee. Keep your chest up, and have your hands on your knees or in prayer position.
- **Child's pose:** in this pose, your toes are touching and your legs are bent, but your knees are spread out as you're reaching forward with your hands. Breathe in and out.
- **Mummy pose (also known as Savasana):** this pose tends to happen at the end of a yoga flow session. It's all about breath, presence, peace, stillness, and welcoming new energy. This reminds us that we are divine beings and that resting is a portal to another

BREATHE

CACTUS POSE
OF SELKET

HAPPY BABY
POSE

NEFERTUM
POSE

CHILD'S
POSE

mummy /
SAVASANA POSE

life. It's similar to how the Kemites believed in the afterlife. For the Kemites, life really started once a person died, and everything they did while alive was in honor of the new life they hoped to experience after death. The Mummy pose is a reminder of this cycle of rebirth.

"Our last pose is an extra fun pose I made up last week," said Ascension Adam, filled with pride. "The Baobab Tree pose. It's like the Tree pose, but I love baobabs, so I changed the name."

Baobab trees are the most mystical and mysterious of all African trees. They're some of the oldest trees in the world and can live up to five thousand years, which is why they're often called "The Tree of Life." They can grow up to ninety-eight feet tall and be thirty-six feet in diameter. Baobab trees are locally known as "renala" in Madagascar (an island off the coast of East Africa), which means *queens of the forest*. Baobabs are found in thirty-two African countries, including Sénégal, Togo, South Africa, and Burkina Faso. The baobab tree also produces incredibly nutritious fruit called "cream of tartar fruit" or "monkey bread."

"My Baobab Tree pose is basically the typical Tree pose, but when you do it, in your mind's eye, imagine your spirit five thousand years from now, still part of the cosmic dance we call life. Stretch your arms up to the sky while bending one of your legs and placing the foot on top of the inner thigh of your standing leg. Stay balanced, like the baobab tree. After a few seconds or minutes of balance, switch sides. Repeat as needed. Think about the fruit you will contribute to the world, just as the baobab does. Your unique energy is a gift to the cosmos. Doing this pose gives us even more life."

Ŋunya, adzido ye, asi me trɔ na ɖoe.
"Nunya, adidoe, asi metunee o."
Wisdom is like a baobab tree;
no one individual can embrace it.

—EWE PROVERB

"Tell me, Forest Scholars, what lessons have you learned from the forest and Forest Magic School so far?" Ascension Adam asked as the group completed their Mummy pose—the final resting pose and a time for meditation.

The scholars took turns sharing what they had learned about papyrus, the Ori, and the power of our breath, presence, and patience.

"Wow. You're already quite knowledgeable about African spirituality. I'm grateful to have shared space and presence with you," Adam said as he poured them homemade tamarind juice, champola de tamarindo. "Always remember, friends, there are many paths in the forest, and many layers to African spirituality, just as there are many poses in Kemetic yoga and many forms of meditation. But instead of getting overwhelmed with all the paths, simply begin down one if you want to get somewhere. Begin to be more mindful of your breath, your posture, your stretches, and your meditations. Begin to treat your body like a temple, just as our Kemetic ancestors did. Begin to tap into your ancestral knowledge by being still."

Cosmic Considerations from Ascension Adam

1. **Prayer:** If you feel called, practice regular prayer. Pray for yourself. Your planet. Your pet. Pray for your parents, grand-parents, and ancestors. Your friends and future. Pray for experiences that have happened and events that will happen. Ask for direction, protection, and safety. Let your Ori guide you.

2. **Study:** Get curious about language, spirituality, philosophy, and art.

3. **Meditation and movement:** Meditation begins with being mindful about what you eat and how you eat. Consistent movement keeps one healthy and young.

4. **Spiritual discipline:** Show up for yourself *every day*. Keep promises to yourself.

5. **Yoga helps us control our breathing:** This skill is useful in dangerous situations as well as in exciting ones.

6. **View one's life as a daily ritual or ceremony:** Have values that you decide to stick with each day. It will help you feel confident and aligned.

As Growth Work, Ascension Adam invited the scholars to research the **forty-two laws of the Kemetic Goddess Ma'at** using their SpacePads and to write down their favorite laws in their papyrus journals. He explained that the Goddess Ma'at symbolizes justice, harmony, truth, balance, equality, order, and love.

Growth Work

Using your own research tools, you also can study the teachings of Goddess Ma'at and write down what you learn in your journal. Remember to use your own Ori as your guide when deciding which teachings speak to you most, and why.

CHAPTER 3

The Sun, Melanin, and the Elements

I t was week three of Forest Magic School, and the scholars were learning about the power of melanin. Melanin is a pigment that gives color to skin and eyes and helps protect it from damage by ultraviolet light.

Facts About Melanin

• We all have melanin within us. It is produced in melanocytes, which are present in different parts of your body such as your skin, eyes, and hair.

Some humans or animals have albinism, which is a reduced amount of melanin pigment, causing them to have very pale skin, hair, and eyes. However, they, too, can feel the power of melanin magic because all humans have neuromelanin, which is the melanin found in your brain and made from different chemical structures than the melanin found in your skin. The amount of neuromelanin you have has no correlation with the pigment (color or shade) of your skin. That means that every human can tap into their melanin magic, and ideally all humans will respect melanated beings, ranging from the darkest to the lightest.

• People with the darkest skin have a higher concentration of melanin. Their melanosomes have a deeper pigment and are in higher numbers, and this is what makes their skin darker.

• Melanin protects you against cell damage that can come from ultraviolet light.

• All humans have about the same amount of melanocytes in their body, even though skin tone varies greatly.

• Vitamins A and E increase melanin.

• Did you know that melanin can also conduct electricity? And that it's present in plants and food, too?

Tata Soleil, the forest scholars' science teacher, had invited them to look for vintage media sources that explained the power of the sun and melanin. The scholars spent the week in deep research mode, with books and their SpacePads. Through his investigations, Kossi had pulled up a piece of knowledge that dated back to a researcher and media personality known as Bill Nye the Science Guy.

"Forest friends, check this out!" Kossi shared excitedly. He played the video from his SpacePad, and his classmates gathered around to watch and listen to what the Science Guy, Bill, had to say.

The scientist showed a map of the continents of earth and pointed to the different amounts of ultraviolet (UV) light landing on each part of the planet. He explained that the intensity of the UV light had to do with how close it was to the equator. He then showed the continent of Africa and highlighted how every human on earth descended from that continent.

Kossi paused the video and explained the rest himself: "The color of different humans' skin changed based on where they moved around the world. We're all one species, but some of us have more melanin than others, and that's why our skin tones are different."

"This guy basically said what Tata Soleil's been explaining all week," said Ife. "We are the source. Every human came from the African continent. It's the root of all humanity. And guess what else? I read in an encyclopedia that Africa's original name is Alkebulan, which means *Mother of humankind* or *Garden of Eden*."

"Yes! Africans are also indigenous beings, just as there are indigenous beings in lands we now call the United States, Mexico, and Brazil," Tata Soleil chimed in.

"What does indigenous mean?" Kossi asked.

"Indigenous refers to something that originates or occurs in a native place. It's what exists at the root of our natures," explained Tata Soleil. "The first human's bones were found in Ethiopia, in East Africa. Some scientists refer to this first human as Lucy, but her native name is Dinkenesh, which means *you are marvelous*. To better understand our spiritual natures, we must study the main spiritual principles found in the motherland and in ourselves. Melanin magic is all around us. It's at the root of who we are."

Tata Soleil loved melanin. She loved the melanin in her skin, she loved studying the benefits of melanin, and she loved sharing her thoughts on melanin with anyone who wanted to listen. She loved melanin so much that a scholar couldn't help but want to take notes about all the cool facts.

"Our melanin has an interesting relationship with the sun," Tata Soleil explained. "It knows that the sun is an essential energy source, but melanin also protects us from the sun's harsher rays. Many African cultures honor the sun and view it as a representation of the cycles of life. As the sun rises and sets each day, our body's rhythms are connected to that cycle. The sun is like a cosmic superhero of sorts. And when we are aware of our melanin magic, we can become superheroes, too."

The scholars pulled out their papyrus journals and wrote down their learnings from what Tata Soleil revealed.

The Power of the Sun in African Spirituality

- The sun acts as an energy source for you to tap into with intention and moderation.
- The sun is an agricultural tool that helps plants grow and provides life to living beings.
- The sun helps activate your inner essence and awareness. This is why celebrating your birthday (one trip around the sun) is significant, because you evolve each year with the sun's help. A fun fact about birthdays: The Kemites were the first to celebrate them. At first these celebrations were limited to Kemetic royalty, but they eventually became a common celebration throughout humanity.

During their lunch break, the forest scholars spent the afternoon sunbathing—in moderation. Their bodies and minds felt recharged by the sun's energy. As they lay down on the red earth near their school, the earth seemed to murmur to them. It was as if they could feel the earth's heartbeat as the sun's rays warmed their melanated skin.

"Looking at the sky feels like a portal," Yawa told her younger brother a few minutes into their sun meditation.

"Maybe it is," Kossi said, smiling with his eyes closed. His third eye was tingling. "The ancestral portal."

Then the wind started blowing intensely. The almost-twins knew it was the sky, and their ancestors, agreeing with them.

<center>~~~~~~~~~~</center>

"Young learners, my name is Professor Infinity," the teacher said as they all sat down in the Bamboo Room for their third class of the day. Professor Infinity was a joyful human. There was a twinkle in his eyes that made him look like he always knew a secret he couldn't share with anyone.

"Today, let's explore alchemy," the professor said once the students were all settled in the learning circle. "At our core, we are alchemists—a master of the elements. To be an alchemist, one must be aware of the power of the elements around us. Our ancestors were aware of their powers of alchemy, and you're here to remember and tap into them as they did.

"Being tuned in to any element means including some balance and harmony, because if you have too much of one element, you can become distracted. When you lose your focus, you're more likely to make mistakes, become impatient with yourself and others, and feel irritated."

Professor Infinity went on to explain that there are several elements in the physical and spiritual world, but the main ones humans interact with are air, fire, water, and earth. In the Dagara culture of the neighboring country of Burkina Faso, there's also the element of minerals. Each of these elements works together, rather than apart, and they're all part of the same whole. They exist within humans spiritually, too. You have the power to tap into them all. And all of them combined create a portal of communication to the spirit world—the ancestral world.

The almost-twins looked at each other at the same time and smiled. They didn't have to utter a word; they telepathically knew what the other was thinking. They both understood why their parents always called Forest Magic School "the ancestral portal." The elements—air, water, earth, minerals, and fire—that were present in the forest, as well as present all around, were spiritual and ancestral.

"Let's travel to the world of air," said Professor Infinity as he opened a window in the Bamboo Room.

The element of air *represents freedom, adventure, travel, self-reflection, intellectual stimulation, communication, and discovery.*

Air provides movement in our lives and in our minds.

In West African spirituality, particularly in the Yorùbá culture, air is a representation of certain **Òrìṣàs** (pronounced *orishas*), such as Oyá and Ṣàngó (pronounced *Shango*)—supernatural beings who control the weather—and also Èṣù (pronounced *Eh-shu*), who controls communication.

The element of air is at play when you hear the leaves rustling in the wind, or when your hair gets blown by a sudden gust. When you fly a kite, or fly in a plane, you're interacting with air.

You use air to breathe, which is its most important purpose. You use it to speak, to sing, and to laugh.

Air is mysterious in that it cannot be seen, but it can certainly be felt. It's also a whole other realm where your ideas are formed. That's why sometimes in school, you are encouraged to "brainstorm" or to draw a "thought cloud."

The more tapped in you are to the element of air—both around you and within you, and through your natal chart (we'll learn more about what that is soon)—the more clearly you're able to think, create, and communicate.

Air also is a bridge between the different elements, such as fire and water.

African Air Gods & Goddesses

Ma'at (Kemet), Oyá (Yorùbá), Aido Wedo (Bénin and Haiti), Èṣù (Yorùbá)

AIR RITUALS

- Literally blowing off steam—let your excess energy out in a safe and freeing way. Such as:
  - Blowing bubbles
  - Flying a kite
  - Running (this can make you feel as if you're flying)
  - Riding in an airplane or hot-air balloon while admiring and greeting the clouds around you
  - Screaming or singing loudly in a safe place, ideally outside or with an open window, to let out any frustrations

"Welcome to the world of fire," the professor continued as he turned on a lava lamp.

Fire is for fuel and force. Optimism. Joy. Laughter. Expansion. Risks. Anger. Jealousy. Action.

The element of fire *represents courage, boldness, warmth, creativity, and passion.*

The sun is the biggest and most constant representation of the element of fire, but every time you gather around a bonfire, as the forest scholars do for story time each Wednesday, you are also in the presence of fire. Even the warm showers you may enjoy taking on cooler nights are a representation of fire, as the water is warmed from the heat.

Fire is a motivating element. It can also be a dangerous one, as all elements have the potential to be (earthquakes, tsunamis, inflamed forests, hurricanes). But in African spirituality, all natural phenomena have a spiritual meaning. They're earth's cry for attention.

Fire's flames can destroy towns and can also nourish and warm households. There's power in that duality. This also represents your own anger—there are times when you may be boiling deep within like a volcano that's about to erupt, and other times when you mask the anger.

Fire is the element you tap into when you want to feel courage. Even just a few minutes of sunbathing can increase your joy and over-all energy. It helps reveal your true desires to you, too.

It's through tapping into the element of fire that you can increase your **vitality** and direct your energy toward your passions and goals.

One of the best representations of fire energy is the phoenix: the mythical bird that turns itself into ash when it's ready for a fresh start, and then proceeds to rise from its own ashes, born anew. Whenever you feel defeated, you can remember the phoenix and, like a magical bird, start over again.

African Fire Gods & Goddesses

Oyá and Ṣàngó (Yorùbá), Sekhmet (Kemet)

FIRE/CANDLE-WORK RITUALS
(ONLY DO THIS WITH PARENTAL OR ADULT SUPERVISION)
- **White candle:** light a white candle when you're ready to release a chapter or begin a new one.
- **Red candle:** light a red candle to call more courage, passion, and confidence into your life.

- **Green candle:** light a green candle to tap into nature's abundance and to increase your own.
- **Black candle:** light a black candle when you want to better understand hidden parts of life or of your own self.
- **Yellow candle:** light a yellow candle when you're ready to forgive, perform, or be reborn.

Tips for dousing the candle: It's best to not blow to take out the flame, but rather use a candle stopper (with the help of an adult) to stop the flame. This maintains the energetic intention of your prayer and releases the ritual.

Full moon release ritual: This is especially true when the moon is in Aries, Sagittarius, or Leo or if you have a lot of fire energy in your birth chart (see chapter 4 to learn about your birth chart). Write down everything you're ready to release. It could be your fears, your imperfections, your sorrows, your guilt, your mistakes, your hardships, your disappointments, your fake friends, or your own petty attitudes. Then burn the paper under the light of the full moon.

"We're now in the wonderland of water," remarked Professor Infinity as droplets of rain tapped against the Bamboo Room's outer walls.

The element of water *represents emotions, love, intuition, cleansing, purifying, immersing oneself, floating, trusting, clarity, compassion, instinct, empathy, self-trust, the womb which housed us when we were in our mother's bellies, protection, forgiveness, and the sacred.*

Do you ever notice how peaceful you feel when you're near sacred bodies of water? Spending time near water can help purify and calm you on a spiritual and physical level. You are 60 percent to 70 percent water, and the fact that water is so present in your body means that you are more sensitive than you may realize. Spending time near water may highlight that sensitivity. Since flowing water represents love, that means you are also love. Imagine your spirit as a constantly flowing waterfall of love. That's what you are.

Just as the oceans' tides change from calm to chaotic, your emotional nature fluctuates in intensity, too. And there's also a mysterious and unknown side to water. (Did you know that 95 percent of the earth's oceans remain unexplored?) Water reminds you to remain curious about what is unexplored within yourself, while also knowing that everything you're meant to know will be revealed when the time is right.

African Water Gods & Goddesses

Ọṣun, Oyá, Yemọja, Olókun, Ṣàngó, Hathor (Ancient Egypt)

HEALING RITUALS WITH WATER

- Take regular cleansing baths, either at home or in a body of water you feel familiar with.
- Make sure to drink filtered, pure water (as pure as you and your caregivers can get it); even try to have a filter when it comes to your sink or shower water.
- Bless your water before drinking it. Tell it words of praise. Water is vibrational, so when you drink it, it has healing properties.
- Protect and honor sources of water.
- Pour water (even coconut water) onto one's Ori.
- Leave a glass of water outside if you've had a bad dream or feel like someone's negative energy is influencing you. Then pour the water out the next day.
- Leave a glass of water on your altar and replace it weekly.

- Be present at a waterfall (with a parent or guardian), and be grateful for the abundance and ever-flowing gifts of nature.
- Speak to the river (Ọṣun/Yemoja), and let her know your feelings.
- Do lake or ocean meditations. This looks like spending time near your favorite body of water and observing the currents. Remember that your body is made up primarily of water, so the water near you reflects the water within you.
- Envision yourself washing away your stress or angst in the shower, and release it as it goes down the drain.
- Learn how to swim, especially as a descendant of Africans, because it's healing the generational relationship with water. Millions of our ancestors lost their lives during the enslavement trade as they were forced across the Atlantic Ocean. There's a lot of trauma that may exist in your ancestors' bodies and that may have been passed down to you. But there's also a lot of joy and healing. When you choose to overcome generational trauma by doing activities that connect you to water, you not only heal yourself, but you also heal all the people who came before you.

"Let's ground ourselves in earth," suggested Professor Infinity as he planted a seed in a pot filled with soil.

The element of earth *represents grounding, meditating, burying, planting seeds, earthing, creating havens, physical touch, and regenerating.*

In the book *The Healing Wisdom of Africa*, author Malidoma Patrice Somé explains how important the six senses are when it comes to the elements. Touch is very grounding. Every time you give someone a hug or a kiss (with their consent), it's a physical exchange that your spirits need to thrive. Humans who live in community, who live near nature, and who receive regular hugs tend to live longer, fuller lives.

Earth represents abundance, stability, security, and determination. It can represent material resources, such as the cozy and spacious cabin house that Papi built with his bare hands, along with the help of the village, thirty-five years ago.

The element of earth represents the ancestral trees that tower around, as well as the seed from which that tree emerged.

Earth is more than the planet on which you live. It's the ground on which you walk, the leaves that you eat, and what you use to purify and scent yourself with.

WAYS TO CONNECT TO EARTH

- Walk barefoot on soil, sand, grass, or granite. Letting the soles of your feet regularly touch the earth helps your blood flow better, which keeps you healthy. It also is a powerful way to fight off viruses, keep your immune system strong, improve your sleep patterns, and keep your body from feeling too "full." What many people call "earthing" is an ancient African practice that is still commonly used on the African continent, especially in villages where most people walk barefoot and are directly connected to Source. Source is the energy that connects all living and nonliving beings, objects, thoughts, dreams, and experiences. Source can also be viewed as "the creator," or if you practice a certain religion, source can be viewed as the supreme being aligned with your spiritual beliefs. Source is the energy that keeps us all here.
- Eat vegetables, especially dark, leafy greens such as spinach, asparagus, and okra.
- Plant fruit, vegetables, flowers, and trees in your garden or a community garden.

Exercise also grounds you. But exercise, like most activities, takes multiple elements. The sweat can represent the water and fire together, because your body gets warmer as you move around and releases water droplets (sweat). You move your body on earth, grounding yourself through sport. But the movement itself is aided by the element of air. And you replenish your energy stores through hydrating before, during, and after any activity with pure water. It takes a village!

African Earth Gods & Goddesses

Asa Yaa (the Akan of Ghana and Côte d'Ivoire), Mawu (Fon and Ewe culture), Oyá (the forest and cemeteries)

EARTH RITUALS

- Burying a loved one or a pet after they've passed away or gone to the afterlife
- Planting seeds for new plants, flowers, and vegetables to bloom and grow
- Taking regular mud clay baths to remove toxins from your body and purify yourself
- Picking up litter from the earth, whether it's yours or someone else's
- Thanking the earth for providing you, your loved ones, and humanity with a home
- Walking barefoot outdoors, because it helps you learn to trust the earth—and that helps you trust yourself and others

After their class on the elements, and right around sunset, the forest scholars headed to story time at the bonfire. This bonfire happened every Wednesday night, and all the villagers, including Mami and Papi, gathered around to speak about the successes and challenges of the day.

The wind (air) blew through their hair as the flames (fire) warmed their bodies. The sound of the drums (earth) reverberated through the night sky as the bats flew above them. Then, right after they had shared their stories from the day, the scholars felt droplets of rain (water) falling onto their Oris. They started dancing, a ritual done in the forest village to thank the universe whenever it rained. All the elements were present with them that night, blessing them.

Growth Work

Brainstorm ways you can better respect and honor each of the elements. For example, Kossi and Yawa noticed that whenever they ate lunch at the forest school cafeteria, they were served their food on large palm leaves for their plates, to minimize the number of dishes that needed cleaning. The forest scholars washed their hands before their meals and used their hands to eat most meals. These actions connected them to the element earth. In what ways do you interact with the different elements? Which ways are eco-friendly (meaning you contribute to keeping earth clean and safe for everyone)?

CHAPTER 4

The Cosmos Within You

The fourth week of Forest Magic School the scholars were awoken by the sounds of crowing roosters. This week they were set to learn about honoring cosmic cycles. The almost-twins were even more excited that morning because it was Mami's birthday.

"She's a Cancer sun," Yawa reminded Kossi as they made their way to the village's artisan market to find a gift for their maternal grandmother. "And she has a Libra moon," Kossi added as he parked his bike near a fig tree.

"Since she's a Cancer sun sign, she'll probably love something that makes her emotional," Yawa said.

"But with her Libra moon, she'd also want a gift that helps her learn something new," Kossi continued. The almost-twins decided to get her a photo album and a new book.

Yawa and Kossi's parents had introduced them to astrology when they were babies by framing a natal report above both of their beds, so they could feel their Ori's connection to it.

Astrology is the oldest form of spirituality known to humans. For many centuries, astronomers—people who study the stars and planets—used to also practice astrology, which is the study of the planets' placements in our solar system and the influence those planets have on earthly affairs. Many astronomers used astrology to help rulers and leaders plan their next moves, using that person's birth chart as a guiding and enlightening tool.

A birth chart is a map of the sky at the exact time, place, and location of your birth, or more specifically, the first breath you took on earth. Every human has one, but not everyone knows about this. Your birth chart is as unique as a snowflake, and no birth chart is the same, not even that of identical twins (kind of like your Ori).

Key Components of a Birth Chart

The planets: in astrology, each planet in our solar system represents a core part of your personality. The Kemites, and other astronomers around the world, studied the planets for several thousands of years and were able to figure out what each represents in a person's birth chart. Here's a short overview:

The sun: the sun is considered a planet in astrology and can also be called a **luminary**. It is the core of your essence. Your sun sign symbolizes the constellation through which the sun was traveling when you were born.

The moon: the moon is considered a planet in astrology or a luminary. It represents your emotional nature. Study your moon sign to know how you best express your feelings, and how you would like to be treated and cared for. It symbolizes how you feel when no one's around.

Mercury: this is the planet of communication. Study your Mercury placement for tips on how best to learn, study, explore, read, write, and communicate. It can also help you figure out which subjects you like most at school, or what job you'd like to have as you keep growing.

Venus: this is the planet of love. Your Venus sign helps you figure out what type of friend you are, and if one day you want to be someone's romantic partner, Venus can help you see the type of person you are drawn to and feel most yourself with.

Mars: this is the planet of action. Your Mars sign shows you what you need to feel good about yourself. It also shows you how you tend to act and who you may be drawn to as a friend, crush, or creative partner.

Jupiter: this is the planet of luck and abundance and the largest planet in our solar system. Its placement in your chart shows you what you need to feel happy in life. But it also shows you ways that you take things to extremes, such as if you eat too much sugar or stay up too late.

Saturn: this is the planet of challenge and responsibility and often has the reputation of being the meanest, coldest, and most difficult planet of all. Saturn has tough-love energy and feels less welcoming than Jupiter. Saturn can teach you in loving ways, if you're willing to do the work and are not afraid of facing challenges. That's when Saturn is the kindest to you, because you're willing to help yourself thrive.

Uranus: this is the planet of change and revolution. It's farther out than the earlier planets, so you may not feel its energies as directly. But it helps you learn to deal with what seems out of your control.

Neptune: this is the planet of dreams, music, movies, and fantasy. It's about what is felt, not seen. Neptune in your chart shows you the type of dream world you want to create.

Pluto: this is the planet of transformation and the farthest in our solar system (in astrology, Pluto is still considered a planet). It's also the most mysterious. Pluto represents all the hidden aspects of yourself. It encourages you to get to know the parts of yourself that you tend to hide from the world. Your Pluto sign also shows you what you need to transform in yourself and in your life.

Rising Sign/Ascendant

This can be calculated only by knowing your exact time of birth. It explains the way people view you from an outsider's perspective. But once they get to know you more deeply, the energy from your sun and moon signs shines through. Your rising sign represents the way people may think you act, even if it's different from how you feel you act.

The Signs

There are twelve zodiac signs in the current astrology system (but keep in mind that the Kemites recorded way more than twelve signs on their temple walls). You'll learn a bit about what each sign represents in modern astrology, but remember that you are *way* more than just your sun sign. So look at your birth chart (you can calculate it for free online with an adult's help) to see what other signs exist there, and read their meanings, too. You are a multidimensional being, and that's super cool!

Aries (March 21 to April 19): the first sign of the zodiac, Aries energy is fierce, passionate, hardworking, and at times selfish. Aries is ruled by Mars and represented by the element fire. Having Aries placements in your chart (especially as your sun, moon, rising, Mercury, Venus, or Mars sign) makes you a natural leader and a confident warrior.

Taurus (April 20 to May 20): the second sign of the zodiac, Taurus energy is fixed, stubborn, and intense. Taurus beings can go to extremes. They can be super calm one second and easily angered the next. Taurus is an earth sign ruled by the planet Venus and loves what makes them feel good, such as delicious food, hilarious movies, and great music.

Gemini (May 21 to June 20): the third sign of the zodiac, Gemini is an air sign ruled by Mercury and represented by the Twins. Gemini energy is always changing. Geminis enjoy traveling and talking. If you have this energy in your birth chart, you may find your mind is always racing with ideas. You can get easily distracted, and you are multitalented, making you curious about what life has to offer.

Cancer (June 21 to July 22): the fourth sign of the zodiac, Cancer is a sensitive water sign ruled by the moon. Since the moon changes signs every two and a half days, Cancers can sometimes be viewed as moody.

But the truth is that if you have Cancer placements, you are a deeply emotional person. You can also be fiercely protective of those you love, which is why you are represented with the crab—you may have a hard outer shell, but you feel strongly inside.

Leo (July 23 to August 22): the fifth sign of the zodiac, Leo is a fire sign ruled by the sun. Leo energy grabs your attention immediately. It's bold and confident. Leo tends to enjoy being in the limelight, or at least being the one calling the shots. Sometimes Leo gets too bossy, though, so compromise is key. If you have Leo energy in your chart, chances are you were born to perform. Let your light shine brightly.

Virgo (August 23 to September 22): the sixth sign of the zodiac, Virgo is an earth sign ruled by Mercury. Virgo energy tends to be more reserved. If you have Virgo energy, you like to plan ahead and often move in silence. You can also be very hard on yourself and on those you love, so it's important to learn how to take a breath and relax.

Libra (September 23 to October 22): the seventh sign of the zodiac, Libra is an air sign ruled by Venus. Like Taurus, Libras love beautiful, great-smelling pleasures. But Libras aren't usually as stubborn or extreme as Taurus. Libra is represented by scales, which means they seek harmony, peace, and warm vibes. One of Libra's lessons is to try to please people too much, especially if it's not good for them.

Scorpio (October 23 to November 21): the eighth sign of the zodiac, Scorpio is a water sign ruled by two planets: Mars and Pluto. Scorpio is the most misunderstood and complicated of all the signs. Should you have Scorpio energy, you can get really angry and can say super mean statements when you feel hurt (like all humans can). But most of the time, Scorpios are looking for love, attention, and understanding, and when they receive that, they become super sweet, using their powerful emotions to change the world.

 Sagittarius (November 22 to December 21): the ninth sign of the zodiac, Sagittarius is a fire sign ruled by Jupiter, which is the planet of expansion. Sagittarius energy tends to be optimistic: If you have this, you look at the positive side of situations and don't let challenges get you down. You may also really love freedom. You don't like when others tell you what to do. If you have Sagittarius energy in your birth chart, you probably should find ways to let out all your fierce energy, perhaps by playing a sport or finding a hobby you enjoy.

 Capricorn (December 22 to January 19): the tenth sign of the zodiac, Capricorn is an earth sign ruled by Saturn, the planet of challenge. Capricorn energy tends to be serious, and sometimes others feel nervous around Capricorns because it's hard to tell what they are feeling. Capricorns take time to open up and trust people. But once someone earns their trust, Capricorn is a warm and true friend.

 Aquarius (January 20 to February 18): the eleventh sign of the zodiac, Aquarius is an air sign ruled by Saturn and by the planet Uranus. Aquarius tends to be ahead of the crowd, often thinking of solutions for problems that will take other people years to come up with. If you have Aquarius energy, you might act like you know everything, so you should remind yourself to listen and learn from others. You don't always need to be the teacher.

Pisces (February 19 to March 20): the twelfth and last sign of the zodiac, Pisces is a water sign ruled by the planets Jupiter and Neptune. Pisces is about dreaming big. If you are a Pisces, you love to dream, to create, and to inspire. Sometimes you feel your emotions so strongly that it feels like a wave that's about to crash over you. You can also take on the emotions of people around you, which is why it's super important for you to protect your energy and to learn the power of saying no.

A birth chart is a gift from the cosmos that people can keep learning from and returning to. Yawa and Kossi already knew their sun, moon, and rising signs by heart. The almost-twins were both Gemini suns. Yawa's moon sign was in Capricorn, and Kossi's moon sign was in Pisces. Yawa's rising sign was Sagittarius, and Kossi's rising sign was Scorpio.

Even though both Yawa and Kossi's core nature (sun sign) was Gemini, which made them appear curious, friendly, and beings who loved traveling, their moon signs showed a more serious (Capricorn) and creative (Pisces) nature. And the first impression people had of Yawa was that she was an adventurer (Sagittarius rising), while Kossi was viewed as an old soul (Scorpio rising).

This is just the beginning of understanding one's birth chart. Your full birth chart is even more complex, but knowing your sun, moon, and rising sign is a great first step. There are also house placements and astrological aspects that make the exploration of our charts even cooler. If you want to be an astrologer, be patient and present with your own birth chart (and the charts of others) and put the different pieces together like a puzzle.

What's your sun, moon, and rising sign, Forest Scholar? Ask a trusted adult who knows about astrology to help you find this magical information using the resources at the end of this book.

"When I was a child living in the United States," Professor Infinity said to the scholars, "I went to an international school, and when I was about your age, my Latin professor helped me plan a toga party, where the students dressed up as the ancient Greek gods and goddesses. I chose Aphrodite, the Greek goddess of beauty.

"But when I grew up and returned to the motherland, I learned through my studies that before Aphrodite, and before the Greek gods and goddesses, there were the Yorùbá Òrìṣàs and the Kemetic deities. The Yorùbá people have connections to Kemet because many of their ancestors migrated out of Ancient Egypt and made their way to Yorùbáland. That's why there are many similarities between West African spirituality and Kemetic spirituality. All forms of African spirituality are connected by a common cultural thread, even if specific parts of each culture make them different, too."

The scholars learned that the Romans and Greeks came to Kemet to study astronomy and astrology. The Romans and Greeks were inspired by and appropriated ancient African gods and goddesses. Appropriation is when a dominant cultural group takes pieces of another group's heritage or cultural makeup and then makes it part of their own, often without giving credit to the original culture.

Professor Infinity continued: "In Kemet, they didn't use the term 'gods and goddesses' as we use today. They used the word *neturu* instead, which means nature. Gods and goddesses are linked to nature. This reminds us that the closer we are to nature, the closer we are to source and to our own powers of creation.

"There's a difference between being inspired by Kemetic culture and simply copying it, or even worse—trying to erase it," Professor

Infinity reminded the scholars. "Forest friends, we must never let any-one erase the rich history of Africa and our spirituality. Africa is the source.

"When I got my certification in teaching African spirituality," their professor continued, "I made a promise to always reveal the roots and wisdom of the Òrìṣàs. This is why we have our Òrìṣà party each year. So next Friday, on Oṣun's day, we'll all dress up as our favorite Òrìṣà, and we'll do a show-and-tell of what we've learned about them. Use this week to start preparing for the party. Make sure to bring your Òrìṣà's favorite meal with you next Friday as an offering to the forest."

"Who's my Òrìṣà?" Clémentine asked Professor Infinity as the for-est scholars started packing up.

"To find that out, you'll have to do an Ifá consultation with your par-ents' or guardians' consent. An Ifá priest or priestess called a 'babalawo' or 'iyánifá' will communicate with your ancestors, and together, they will tell you. Babalawos and iyánifás went through an intense training and learning period before being allowed to share their gifts and per-form Ifá consultations."

"What's an Ifá consultation?"

"It's a reading that helps you connect with your ancestors and ask for guidance and protection in your life. Through that reading, ances-tral spirits can reveal the past, present, and future. It provides you with tools to make decisions that will benefit you and your spiritual health."

The scholars still had many questions, but they remembered how *patience and presence* were keys to learning about African spirituality. So they were patient. And present.

"Before we get to that," Professor Infinity shared as he poured the class some ginger and bissap juice for their snack time, "let me tell you about how the Yorùbá view the world's creation story. Some people call this a myth, but I like to call it an origin story. The world has several origin stories, and it's always fun to discover new ones and see what we can draw from them. All religions and spiritual beliefs come from the same source, so it's important for us to get curious about and respect them. Gather around, forest friends."

The scholars learned about the Yorùbá origin story, which started with the creator, Olódùmarè.

Olódùmarè sent supernatural forces of nature, called Òrìṣàs, down to earth. Each spirit had a special ability and ruled specific aspects of nature and life. They founded communities and were always connected to both the earth and the sky realms. There are 401 Òrìṣàs, however the ten most known ones are:

1. **Obatalá:** the elder Òrìṣà of creation and peace
2. **Yemọja:** the Òrìṣà of the seas and the moon; the mother of all Òrìṣàs
3. **Oyá:** the Òrìṣà of storms, magic, rebirth, and the forests
4. **Ọṣun:** the Òrìṣà of love, beauty, children, and rivers
5. **Ọ̀rúnmìlà:** the Òrìṣà of wisdom, spirituality, and destiny
6. **Èṣù:** the Òrìṣà of crossroads, communication, and the marketplace
7. **Ògún:** the Òrìṣà of action, iron, fire, and war
8. **Ọbalúayé:** the Òrìṣà of challenge and healing
9. **Ṣàngó:** the Òrìṣà of lightning and revolution
10. **Olókun:** the Òrìṣà of the deep seas

In Yorùbá spirituality, your Ori (divine head) is ruled by an Òrìṣà, and as you connect to that Òrìṣà and learn more about them, you become a more powerful human being and feel more connected to both the earth and the skies. In a way, humans are Òrìṣàs, too.

Even today, there are tall plank African masks such as some found in Dogo, Mali, representing the connection between the Òrìṣàs and the earth. They're viewed as cosmic connectors, and they are a bridge between earth and the heavens.

"Now it's your turn to do some research, scholars," Professor Infinity said. "Have fun choosing and studying an Òrìsà to embody. Take your time to explore, and let's regroup at the party next week to share our findings."

For Growth Work, the scholars each had to find out their Òrìsà, or choose their favorite and do research on them, using a combination of advice from elders in the village, their SpacePads (in moderation), and their own Oris. The Òrìsà party on Friday would be in the center of the village, where each scholar would present on a stage.

You can also research the Òrìsàs if you feel called, Forest Scholar. Which one speaks to you most, and why?

Once back in their grandparents' home, Yawa and Kossi found out more about the Òrìsàs via the research of Nigerian culture journalist and photographer Folu Oyefeso. Reading his insights made them feel as if they were traveling through the world of Yorùbá spirituality. They also found a book on Mami and Papi's bookshelf called *Signs & Skymates*. They looked through it with their grandparents and explored the connection the author had made between the Òrìsàs and the modern-day planetary names and energies.

As Mami made the almost-twins aware of the connections between both, she said, "We're reclaiming the origins of this cosmic practice by knowing the indigenous roots of the current planetary names. And at the Òrìsà party, you can let everyone know the Yorùbá connections in your birth chart."

Kossi and Yawa were excited about this journey of remembrance, and they were glad Mami was there to help them. They pulled out their papyrus journals and got to work studying and planning for the party next week. They weren't the only ones excited—the Òrìsàs were, too!

The Chakras in African Spirituality

"Did you know that while chakras are often associated as being of Indian descent, they also have Yorùbá origins?" Papi asked the almost-twins that weekend as they were chopping plantains in the kitchen for dinner. Papi had overheard the almost-twins talking to Mami about the Òrìsàs, and he was glad his grandchildren felt connected to them. "Ancient African spiritualists knew about chakras before they were even called chakras. The Yorùbá Òrìsàs can also be viewed as representations of the chakras. These teachings are the basis of our current chakra system."

Chakras, or "heightened energy zones," are sensitive points of focus for meditation. This means you tend to feel more energy in certain parts of your body. Chakras exist in your body and spirit. Chakras are often represented as orbs of energy, or multicolored flowers, where spiritual energy is stored. Tapping into the chakras works best when you visualize the energy points in your body and when you connect them with the deity—Òrìsà—that represents them.

The key is to not view these chakras as separate pieces, but rather as a whole. You must combine their energies into one big source, like your birth chart or like all the elements in the cosmos that work together to keep us alive and well. Feeling connected to all these energy points in your body, mind, and spirit helps you heal yourself and others. The more your chakras are aligned, the better your energy is, and the better life feels!

The Chakras

1. **Ground chakra (root)**
   - Represented by earth
   - Color is red
   - Ògún is the Òrìṣà deity
   - Osiris is the Kemetic god
   - It represents safety, security, pride in one's roots/ancestry, and the need to survive and thrive
   - It is blocked by fear

2. **Water chakra (sacral)**
   - Represented by water
   - Color is orange
   - Yemọja and Mami Wata are the Òrìṣà goddesses
   - Anubis is the Kemetic god
   - It represents pleasure, balanced emotions, feeling good in your body, creativity, and abundance
   - It is blocked by guilt

3. **Fire chakra (solar plexus)**
   - Represented by fire
   - Color is yellow
   - Ṣàngó and Oyá are the Òrìṣà deities
   - Sekhmet is the Kemetic god
   - It represents stepping into our power and making courageous choices
   - It is blocked by shame

4. **Heart chakra**
   - Represented by air
   - Color is green
   - Ọṣun (love) is the Òrìṣà goddess
   - Hathor is the Kemetic goddess
   - It represents the healing power of love, beauty, harmony, peace, and helps you to forgive
   - It is blocked by grief due to experiencing loss

5. **Sound chakra (throat)**
   - Represented by space (the cosmos)
   - Color is blue
   - Oyá is the Òrìṣà goddess
   - Djehuti is the Kemetic god
   - It represents truth, trust, and making smart decisions
   - It is blocked by being dishonest with yourself and lying to yourself or to others

6. **Light or crown chakra (head)**
   - Represented by Ori (divine head)
   - Colors are violet and white
   - Obatalá is the Òrìṣà deity
   - It represents the connection to creation, the power of universal flow, and your changing nature
   - It is blocked by negativity

7. **Third-eye chakra (pure cosmic energy)**
   - Represented by the creator
   - Colors are indigo and royal blue
   - Olódùmarè is the Òrìṣà deity
   - Nut is the Kemetic goddess
   - It represents rebirth and infinite creative energy
   - It is blocked by extreme anxiety

Growth Work

Now that you're familiar with the different chakra points, which chakra do you feel most connected to? Which chakra do you feel less connected to? Why? Reflect on what makes your Ori (divine head or inner knowing) tingle. What is your intuition telling you?

CHAPTER 5

The Òrìṣà Party

T he forest scholars had spent the week preparing for the Òrìṣà party, which occurred on the Friday night of their fifth week of Forest Magic School. The courtyard had been transformed into a performance theater, and the stage was decorated with white and gold curtains, lined with cowries. Everyone looked stunning dressed as their Òrìṣà of choice.

"Welcome to the Òrìṣà party!" said Professor Infinity as the forest scholars, teachers, parents, and grandparents got settled in. "Everyone looks amazing. The energy out here is strong! I know the Òrìṣàs are happy to be so publicly celebrated. Many of you did your research and have connected the modern astrological planets with the Òrìṣàs. We'll therefore present ourselves as our Òrìṣà in the order of the planets and luminaries in our solar system. Without further ado, we call forth the representation of the sun!"

Obatalá = The Sun, the Luminary of Life

Sundiata went first. She rolled her wheelchair up the ramp and took center stage. She was wearing a white flowing dress, with purple and red decorative patterns, which represented Obatalá's diversity of viewpoints and paths. She took a deep breath before beginning, remembering the importance of presence and patience.

"I'm Obatalá, a representation of the sun, which gives energy to all living beings. I'm viewed as the SkyFather, or the elder Òrìsà, because I helped Olódùmarè create the sky and human beings. Fun fact: When Olódùmarè first created humans, they didn't include human heads. I saw how clumsy that made humans, and I suggested that heads be added. So humans have heads now. Oris too.

"I love living at the top of mountains. I'm the one people come to when they need strength, courage, passion, and motivation. I represent justice, leadership, the handicapped, and overcoming challenges. I've experienced much difficulty as a warrior, and I've made many mistakes along the way. I've learned from these mistakes, and now I've chosen the path of peace, calmness, and pure energy. I help fellow Òrìsàs and humans tap into this energy, too, by shining my healing rays of wisdom. My day of the week is Sunday, as it's literally the sun's day. Several of the Òrìsàs are my children, and my amazing wife is Yemoja, empress of the seas. I have both male and female body parts, both feminine and masculine energy. I'm gender-fluid.

"When giving me offerings, keep it simple. White, bland, easy-to-make meals such as rice or bread will make my day. I also like yams, eggs, and coconut. You can pray to me by lighting a white candle (with adult supervision, please), as white is my favorite color. I love all things white: cowries, candles, lace, flowers, seashells, snails, and silver coins and jewelry. The one thing I ask of you when you pray to me or call on me is to be honest with yourself. Tell yourself the truth and tell me the truth. I can see through all lies, and even though I can be nice, I stay away from those who don't have good intentions."

Yemọja = the Moon, the Luminary of Emotions

Yawa took a deep breath before beginning. She looked breathtaking, adorned in a dress made of cowries, looking like the moon surrounded by brilliant stars. That morning, Mami had told Yawa that her Ori was ruled by Yemọja, based on a consultation Yawa's parents had had with an Ifá priestess when Yawa was younger. So this Òrìṣà party was very special to Yawa. In that moment, she felt Yemọja speaking through her.

"Hi, forest friends. It's me, Yemọja, the Òrìṣà of the sea, the oceans, and the moon. The mother of all—Mother Earth. I'm also known as 'the mother whose children are like fish.' I represent the power of the oceans' tides and of your internal navigation system. This is your intuition. Call on me when you want to better know, love, and hear yourself.

"The Yorùbá people celebrate me during a seventeen-day festival in October called 'Odun Yemọja.' But it's not only the Yorùbá of West Africa who honor me. Many beings in Cuba, Brazil, and Eastern Europe respect and celebrate my gifts. My colors are ocean blue and white. I absolutely adore cowries, so you may see me wearing them often.

"Ooh, did you know that I'm also a *mermaid*? I live in mermaid world, which is why some people also call me Mami Wata. If you'd like to give me an offering, I gratefully accept yams, seashells, cowries, white flowers, fruit (especially watermelon), goats, songs, and love. As the mother Òrìṣà, I protect all humans, but especially the youth. My favorite humans are children. That's why parents, and especially mothers, pray to me and ask me to protect their homes and families. You can also pray to me whenever you need help navigating powerful emotions coursing through you. I'm here to help you remember that there is strength in sensitivity.

"Like me, you can choose who you want to be, and when you want to be it. The more you connect to my energy, the more you'll feel in tune with yourself and your inner wisdom. My energy exists in all humans—boys, girls, men, women, and those who transcend gender. I am the mother of all. But I'm not always as sweet as I appear. I can get angry, just like the ocean's waves. This reminds you to also let yourself feel anger and not to hold it in. My special number is seven, and my days of the week are Saturday, and Monday, also known as the moon's day."

Èṣù = Mercury, the Planet of Communication

Kossi came center stage, wearing a black-and-maroon top and matching pants that he had asked a local tonton to sew for him. He had a slightly mischievous twinkle in his eye. That past weekend, Papi had told him that his Ori was ruled by Èṣù, which happened to be Kossi's favorite Òrìṣà. The young god took a deep breath, in and out, then introduced himself.

"I'm Èṣù, the Òrìṣà of communication, the marketplace, and crossroads. I'm one of the first Òrìṣàs to be created, and my energy controls the destiny and fate of humankind. People view me as a trickster because I like to joke, play, and laugh. But I view myself more as an awakener, a magician, and an expert communicator. I'm here to remind you to not take life, or yourself, too seriously. I'm super smart, and I'm a master of languages. In certain indigenous regions of Brazil (such as Salvador da Bahia) and West Africa, you'll see shrines honoring me at different crossroads, representing that I can literally help open (or close) doors. Pray to me when you're traveling or when you have a big speech to give. I am always present, in all prayers.

"I'm also here to remind you of the power of your words. When you choose to speak, write, scream, sing, or express yourself, my energy is with you. Remember that your words can both heal or harm others (and yourself). Choose your words wisely. Whenever there's drama or disagreements in your life, talk to me and ask me to help you find a solution, and I will. I will help you look at life through new perspectives, and I will offer you the opportunity to choose new possibilities. A powerful way to connect with me is to meditate and connect deeply with yourself in nature, while visualizing what you would like to bring forth in your life. I can see your visions and help them come true.

"A divine messenger, I'm known for the ability to transform bad luck into good. But this only happens when I want to. I can also get into trouble and cause other people to get into trouble, too. I have my shadow side. We all do. I'm not perfect, and I don't claim to be. When Africans were enslaved in the Americas, my spirit traveled with them. I served as a source of remembrance. I helped their Ori remember their roots. I can do the same for you if you'd like. Some of my favorite offerings to receive are palm oil, palm wine, salt, pepper, and kola nuts. Monday is my day of the week."

Ọṣun = Venus, the Planet of Love

The young mystic Akua came to the Òrìṣà party as Ọṣun, wearing a flowing yellow dress and a necklace made of sunflowers. Ọṣun's love

shined through her. After taking a deep breath, Akua was present.

"I'm Ọṣun, the Òrìṣà of rivers, love, children, joy, and beauty. I rule pleasurable delights, such as the sweet taste of honey, the beautiful reflection you see when looking in a mirror, and the enchanting sounds of music. Come greet me at the Ọṣun-Òṣogbo sacred grove in Ọṣun State, Nigeria, about a three-hour drive north from the capital of Lagos. The flowing river that you see there is me. You'll also see a statue of me with my arms outstretched in front of the river, as an invitation to love. I send love your way, and you send love my way, too.

"Some of my favorite offerings are honey, sunflowers, fruit, spoons, music, or a mirror to admire myself with. I may come off as sweet, but if I feel that someone is taking advantage of me, I can become fiercely self-protective and shut others out. Kind of like when the other Òrìṣàs didn't take me seriously during the early days on earth. They ignored my contributions and acted as if I didn't matter. So I decided to leave *Aye* (earth) and return to the sky world. As soon as I did that, the earth lost all its vegetation, crops began to die, and everything felt cold and soulless. My fellow Òrìṣàs realized the error of their ways, came up to the skies, and pleaded for me to forgive them and return to earth. Luckily for me, I am a forgiving person, and I loved the attention they showered me with. I forgave them, came back to earth, and the land thrived again.

"My favorite color is yellow or gold, my favorite animal is the peacock, and my special number is five. You can honor me on Fridays, and during the month of August there's a huge festival at my special grove, in Nigeria. Come through and enjoy my peaceful river. I, and my special monkey friends, will greet you and your loved ones with open arms and a pure heart."

Ògún = Mars, the Planet of War

One deep breath later, Ife stood up. He was adorned with a beautiful green kente cloth that he had wrapped around his waist. He wore a

large beaded black necklace over his chest. He was holding an accessory that looked like a blunt blade made from iron and a shield. As he walked up to the stage, everyone could feel his striking power.

"My name is Ògún, and I am the Òrìṣà of iron, action, and passion. I'm one of the first Òrìṣàs to come to earth. Some view me as the Òrìṣà of war, but the truth is, I don't always want to fight. I am aware of the dangers that exist in our spiritual and physical worlds.

I am all about protecting yourself from danger, especially the type you don't see coming. Call on my energy when you have to fight back against injustice—I will give you the courage and drive to overcome, just as I guide and empower humans who take part in revolutionary movements and claim their freedom.

"Many people fear me, but many people also do not understand me. You can recognize me because of my sword or machete, as well as my shield, which I always carry with me. I know how to create materials from iron, so I'm also a blacksmith. I'm not always friends with the other Òrìṣàs, but we do respect one another. Many of them come to me for protection, as do humans all around the world. Tuesday is my day of the week. My symbol is the iroko tree. As offerings, you can gift me kola nuts, salt, yams, water, palm oil, palm wine, and tortoise. My colors are green and black, and my special numbers are three and seven.

"Call on me whenever you need strength getting through a difficult situation. I provide strength both for your body and for your spirit. But since I am the Òrìṣà of action, I am also here to remind you of the importance of being active and moving your body regularly. If you ever get too lazy or fall into the same old routine, grab a basketball, Frisbee, jump rope, or Hula-Hoop, go outside, and move your body in whatever way is accessible to you. Even going for a walk, stroll, or run with your family or friends is a great way to tap into my energy.

"I am a warrior training warriors. View yourself as a warrior, too. It was my warrior energy that helped me restore the sun after it had been stolen by evil spirits. Your warrior energy can brighten even your cloudiest day. I know this because I've made mistakes and I've let my anger get the best of me. I've destroyed villages because I lacked patience and presence with myself and with others. But I was able to own my mistakes, and I was brave enough to try again. Next time you make a mistake, admit it to yourself first, then give yourself permission to try again."

Ọ̀rúnmìlà = Jupiter, the Planet of Luck

Felipe got up next and spoke. Dressed in a green-and-yellow **dashiki**, he resembled a vibrant garden, filled with plants and kissed by sunlight.

"Fellow magicians, I am Ọ̀rúnmìlà, the Òrìṣà of wisdom and blessings. I'm known as the grand priest of knowledge. I am the professor of advanced spiritual insights.

"Obatalá, the SkyFather, is my father. They made me in their image. I'm the only Òrìṣà who was allowed to see when the universe was being created. I was given the power to see into the future and to tell about it. I have psychic abilities, and I know what each human needs to find happiness, health, and well-being. If you listen to my insights and guidance, you will find your way and live a happy life.

"My brothers are Èṣù, Ògún, and Ṣàngó. Ṣàngó works with me to heal the injured. Ọṣun is also a close friend who comes to me for guidance, and who brings healing energy into my life. You can often see me with my **divination** board, shown as a palm tree, one of my favorite places to rest. I am strongly connected to the natural world and to plants. I create healing medicine from plants. My favorite colors are green and yellow, as they connect me to the vibrant energy of the natural world. My special number is sixteen and my day of the week is Monday.

"Some of the animals connected with my energy are the leopard, the parrot, the chameleon, and the iguana. Some of my favorite offerings to receive are delicious cakes, yams, nuts, coconut, candles, and wine. Call on me when you want to get better at listening to your Ori, your inner voice, and your intuition. When you are ready to step into your future, or when you have questions about your past, know that I am here. I will help you quiet the outside noise and better hear who you are."

Obalúayé = Saturn, the Planet of Responsibility

The next person to speak was Professor Infinity, dressed in a vibrant red jumpsuit. He took a deep breath, revealed a knowing smile, and began.

"I'm Obalúayé, the Òrìṣà of wisdom, wellness, healing, and disease. I'm here to help you grow through challenges and to help you view them as a normal part of life. I'm here to help you understand that life isn't always sunny. Sometimes it's somber and sad. I'm here to remind you that you don't always have to figure out your problems on your own. You have the wisdom of the trees, your ancestors, your spirit guides, your friends, and, of course, your Ori. I'm here to teach you how to be more mature and responsible.

"When life gets tough, I probably have something to do with it. Instead of moping and crying about it (well, actually, Yemọja and Ọṣun would probably say you can cry as much as you want), get up and do something about it. At the same time, I'm here to remind you to take your time. *Presence and patience, remember?* Sometimes the reward you're seeking will arrive after a long moment of feeling like you'll never get it.

"I love showing humans and other Òrìṣàs how putting in the work day after day can lead to great blessings and manifestations. Sometimes my energy can heal, and other times it can punish. I am very connected to the medicine world, which is why some people fear me; they never know if I'll bless them with great health or punish them with bad. I am connected to Aye, the earth. As offerings, I accept grains, black-eyed peas, palm wine (emu), and roasted corn. My day of the week is Thursday, and my colors are red, brown, black, and royal purple."

Ṣàngó/Oyá = a joint representation of Uranus, the Planet of Revolution

The forest friends in the audience were absolutely loving this party. Their Oris were tingling. They looked up at the next people approaching. Tata Soleil and Professor Ori arrived wearing red outfits highlighting a warrior nature and carrying lightning bolts. The two forest professors smiled, held hands, took a deep breath, and spoke.

"We are Ṣàngó and Oyá, the Òrìṣàs of lightning, thunder, and the weather. We represent the revolution that exists around and within us. Call on us when you want to be more in tune with your own supernatural abilities or when you want to feel more confident about yourself."

"I represent the changing tides and mysteries of nature," said Oyá. "The weather is quite unpredictable, just like me. Sometimes it's sunny, and other times there are violent winds. Sometimes it drizzles, other times the rain pours nonstop."

"I'm married to the incredible Oyá, who gave me the power to create lightning!" added Sàngó. "Thanks to Oyá, I am the most feared and powerful Òrìṣà of all. You can find me walking with my double axe to warn enemies not to mess with me or my loved ones. If you want to give me offerings, I love red palm oil, yam, crab, and corn. One of my favorite foods ever is amala, a thick paste made of cornmeal, yam, or cassava flour that's often eaten with okra. You can also dance and sing for me as an offering. I have the power to cast magic spells, and I am an excellent drummer. As much as people view me as a fierce warrior, I'm also a romantic and a social butterfly when I want to be. I'm here to remind you to create a balance between work and play. My animal symbols are turtles, roosters, and dogs, and the plant that represents me is the royal palm tree. My special numbers are six and twelve. My day of the week is Friday."

"And mine is Wednesday," Oyá continued, revealing a playful smile. "To honor us, you can wear red or maroon, light red candles, respect the rain, smile at the lightning, express gratitude for the life-giving power of your breath, laugh with the thunder, and dance away your fears or worries. I especially love to dance. It gives me life!"

"When there's a thunderstorm and you see lightning striking, it's most likely because we're in a heated argument," Ṣàngó added, winking at his wife. "But we always find a way to make up, and that's when the weather calms down."

Olókun = Neptune, the Planet of Fantasy, Illusion, and Dreams

Next, Michael appeared wearing white and holding a three-pronged spear called a trident. As he walked, the lower half of his body seemed to shape-shift between legs and a merman's tail. He lay down in the center of the stage and closed his eyes for a solid minute. Then the pensive scholar opened his eyes, took a deep breath in and out, and said:

"I'm Olókun, the Òrìṣà of dreams and the deep seas. I'm who you find in the dreaming world, and in the waking world I assist you and help make your dreams come true. Fishermen and women pray to me (and Yemoja) when they are at sea, and I watch over them. I'm the spirit of the deepest waters of the earth and the ocean floor. I'm just as mysterious and dangerous as the ocean floor, too, and no one really knows who I am or who I have the potential to be. I can show up in female, male, or androgynous forms. Androgynous means having physical traits of both male and female.

"My home is found in the deepest part of the ocean. That is where I feel most at peace. There is a whole other world in the ocean's depths, and I rule that world and all its wonders. I see what most people cannot see. I also serve as a reminder to honor and accept your own darkness, because I live in the darkness. The sun's light has never touched the ocean floor. But still, I shine.

"I can also show up as half fish, half human. People usually fear and respect me because I can turn the oceans' tides against them with the bat of an eye. I can also be as sweet as a flowing river. If you'd like to give me offerings, you can place them directly in the ocean or sea. I gladly accept obi (kola nut), salt, honey, watermelon, papaya, apples, grapes, coconuts, epo pupa (palm oil), green plantains, and black beans. I am represented by the color blue and the numbers seven and nine. My day of the week is Monday. I'm here to help you feel better and more at peace emotionally. I can make your deepest dreams come true if you give yourself permission to fully follow your heart and live out your dreams. I bring great blessings to those who honor me. But I also have the power to destroy everything and every-one on Aye with the power of the element water, of which I am the ruler. So beware."

Oyá = Pluto, the Planet of Transformation and the Afterlife

It was Clémentine's turn to give the final Òrìṣà speech. She wore a deep purple sundress representing how the sky looks right after an intense storm. Clémentine took a deep breath, and the winds in the forest breathed along with her. Then she began.

"I'm Oyá, the Yorùbá Òrìṣà of the winds, lightning, thun-der, storms, waterfalls, and the forest. Not only do I accompany the dead as they transition to the spirit world, but I also assist the newborns as they enter the liv-ing realm. Since I am the Òrìṣà of air, I represent both the first and last breath that beings take on earth. I am the keeper of secrets, surrounded by mystery. Just like the changing weather I rule over, I can be as calm as a gentle breeze or as intense as an overwhelming typhoon. It depends on how I feel. My sister is Yemọja, the mother of the oceans. She helps keep me calm whenever I'm about to lose my temper.

"Call on me when you need to understand life's mysteries, when you're grieving the physical loss of a loved one, or when you're fearing death. I'll be here to remind you of life's changing and regenerating cycles. You can find me protecting ceremonies or called upon during funerals. The Niger River is a representation of me. My colors are red, burgundy, and brown. But royal purple is what I'm most often seen in.

"You can find sculptures of me in the Sacred Forest of Bénin and the cities of Rio de Janeiro and Salvador in Brazil. My animal symbols are bats, butterflies, dragonflies, buffaloes, fireflies, and birds. My favorite foods are chocolate, red wine, chickpeas, purple grapes, beets, eggplants, rice, and black beans. And my day of the week is Wednesday. In Cuba, where many Afro-descendants honor me, I'm celebrated on February 2, which is the second day of the second month of the year. You can find me holding a machete, a blade, or an ax, and using tornadoes as a form of protection. The lightning bolt is also one of my favorite tools of power. It helps illuminate truths that others try to hide from me or from the world.

"Nine is my favorite number, which is why I love wearing nine copper bracelets on my wrist. I am viewed as the Mother of Nine Children, because I had nine, but they all transitioned to the ancestral realm at birth. I know what pain feels like, and I'm here to help you move past life's challenges, one breath at a time."

The forest scholars received a standing ovation. Many of the Forest Magic School professors and the forest scholars' parents also came to the Òrìsà party. Tata Soleil had done an outfit change and was now dressed as Goddess Isis—a nod to the Kemetic origins of many Yorùbá people. Other Kemetic gods and goddesses include:

• **Neith**, the mother of Re. Neith is one of the original goddesses who produced the world. As the Kemetic goddess of creation and wisdom, she rules hunting, weaving, and battles.

• **Osiris**, a god also known as Amun-Re ("The Sun"). Osiris is a form of the sun god. The sphynx (half human, half lion) is one of Osiris's symbols. He's the Kemetic god known for ruling the afterlife.

- **Aset**, also called Isis, is the goddess of healing magic. She even had the power to cast spells on Ra, the sun god, who is her husband. Charming and sweet, Isis is also deeply protective of her loved ones.
- **Horus**, a falcon-shaped god who has a sun or star as his right eye. Horus is the son of Isis and Osiris. Horus is the god of sunlight, protection, the sky, and healing.
- **Hathor**, the goddess of music, healing, women, and the sun. Hathor is viewed as a deity of the skies, similar to Ra.
- **Sekhmet**, the daughter of Ra. Similar to Obalúayé, Sekhmet has the power to heal disease and also to inflict it onto others. Unpredictable and easily angered, she holds powerful abilities that make the other gods and goddesses wary of her.
- **Thoth**, the lunar deity of hieroglyphics and knowledge. He is the god who created writing, wisdom, art, and magic.
- **Sopdet**, a goddess whose name translates as "triangle." This is also the original name of the star called Sirius—the brightest star in our night sky. The Dogon of Mali, some of the first astronomers and astrologers, knew about the Sirius star system before any others. Sopdet has power over life and death, similar to the Yorùbá deity Oyá.

Once the forest scholars had presented themselves as their respective Òrìṣàs, everyone gathered at the dining table on the balcony to celebrate a successful party. They enjoyed the meals, drinks, and offerings that had been brought, and they danced and mingled with joy. As the party neared its end, Professor Infinity was beaming with pride as he proposed a community Growth Work assignment.

Growth Work

Think of all the superheroes you might be familiar with. Are there any that remind you of the Òrìṣàs? For example, Thor, the Marvel superhero of lightning and thunder, seems to be an appropriation of Ṣàngó and Oyá, the Òrìṣàs of lightning and thunder. Look up what Olókun looks like. Does a well-known "god of the seas" from a popular mermaid movie remind you of them? Why do you think that is? With the knowledge you now have, you can also write your own Òrìṣà superhero story in your journal. (Perhaps one day, with your help, we'll watch the stories of the Òrìṣàs, the original superheroes, on the big screen!)

CHAPTER 6
Cosmic Clocks and the Tawe Tree of Time

On the sixth week, the scholars were invited to explore the cosmos around them by wandering throughout the forest and connecting with the elements, the Òrìṣàs, and their own Ori.

"There are numerous ways to communicate with yourself and others, sometimes without the need for words," Professor Ori reminded them.

So the wandering began. The forest friends went on an adventure trek through the forest.

Yawa kept feeling drawn to a certain tree whose lower branches had merged and formed a ropelike bridge. Its roots were strong and its trunk steady, and it looked like it was hundreds of years old. Professor Ori observed Yawa's connection with the tree.

"Looks like you've taken a liking to the Tawe Tree of Time. This tree helps you time travel," the professor said.

"Really? How?" Yawa and Kossi asked in unison.

"By helping you look at time a different way." Professor Ori put their hand on the tree's trunk, took a deep breath, and smiled. Then they sat near the tree, put their back against its trunk, closed their eyes, took deep breaths, and meditated.

The forest scholars sat in silence, focusing on their breathing. Soon their breath seemed to fall into rhythm with the tree's leaves rustling through the wind. Professor Ori opened their eyes and looked at the scholars.

"The Tawe Tree of Time taught me that time is a human invention to help people feel a sense of control. But a clock is not the only way to define or measure time. This experience that you're living, this moment that you're now in, at its simplest—that's time.

"Instead of viewing time as a straight line," the professor continued, "what if you were to view it as a spiral? The Tawe Tree of Time's roots and branches remind us of this."

"What does viewing time as a spiral mean?" Kossi asked. "Is it like when you keep spinning around and then the world feels dizzy for a few seconds?"

The Tawe Tree's branches started swaying passionately in the wind. It seemed to be laughing.

"I hadn't thought of it that way," said Professor Ori. "Yes, that is a form of spiraling. It also makes me think of cycles. Did you know that our ancestors, and many indigenous cultures, followed and still follow a lunar calendar and measured time based on the cycles of the moon? Just as the cycles of the sun and moon influence life on earth, earth is also influenced by the cycles of the cosmos that it calls home.

"And we, forest friends, are part of this larger cycle of existence. The Tawe Tree's roots aren't just her roots. They're connected to the roots of other trees and of other 'times.' All living beings in the forest live in an ecosystem—a community of beings living together and helping one another survive. In the same way that time follows cycles, these ecologies span forward and backward and depend on one another.

"What you can learn from this is that we should live in community with one another and the world around us, instead of as individuals, which is very much what modern society is set up to be like.

"Nature holds memory in the land and the water, and its organisms live and breathe much as we do. We can gather lessons on how to stay rooted and grounded, but also how to be guided by unseen forces. These memories are ancient and will continue to exist through time. You, the trees around you, your ancestors, and your Ori are living in a timeless spiral."

Professor Ori closed their eyes again and breathed deeply, along with the Tawe Tree.

The next day, it was Kossi's turn to choose where the Capsule Tree Portal would take the class.

"My mom's been telling us about how part of our ancestors on Mami's side had previously been enslaved in Brazil before returning to Bénin generations later. Remember, Yawa?"

"Yes, our great-grandma's name is De Campos, which means *of the fields* in Portuguese. Many descendants of formerly enslaved Africans now living in Bénin and Togo have Brazilian last names due to enslavement."

"More than 60 percent of Brazil's population comes from indigenous or African ancestry," Professor Ori explained. "The spiritual beliefs of indigenous and Afro-Brazilians are therefore directly tied to West African spirituality. Most Afro-Brazilians originally were from the regions now known as Ghana, Togo, Côte d'Ivoire, Bénin, Angola, and Nigeria."

"Let's go to Brazil," Kossi said as he approached the capsule tree.

The scholars entered the Tree Capsule Portal and traveled to Brazil, where they met Maryano Maya, an indigenous forest friend living in the city of São Paulo. Maryano Maya's ancestors were the Tupi people of Pindoreta in Brazil and the Mandê people of Mali.

After being welcomed with a delicious cup of coconut water blended with lime, and dancing to the sound of the welcoming drums, just as they did when they arrived at Forest Magic School, the scholars sat in a learning circle in the Brazilian forest.

"Can you tell us more about what it was like growing up in Brazil?" Kossi asked Maryano Maya.

"When I was just a child, my parents would tell me a story called 'Saci Pererê.' It's a well-known Guaraní tale that became Brazilian folklore. I was quite interested in what people had to say about it, since this Saci Pererê is a powerful being of the forest. The Black, or magically melanated, people that grew up with the indigenous of Brazil started to believe in this tale."

"We have forest spirits in Bambo Forest, too," Yawa said as she scooted closer and enjoyed her raw cacao bean.

"Yes, there are many similarities between Brazil and Africa!" Maryano Maya said with pride. "All right, let's begin story time."

The forest scholars learned all about Saci Pererê, also known by the names of Atsui or Yasy Jatere. He's a powerful guardian of the forest. Different cultures have different ways of representing this spirit, but some of his overall features are his incredible powers of the forest. So fast that if you happen to see this spirit in the forest, around the lower part of his body, you will see a tornado instead of his legs. He travels swiftly with the speed of the wind, and he has only one leg. He is either unclothed, or wearing red, depending on where you hear the tale.

"What is he here to do?" Ife wanted to know.

"Saci is responsible for guarding the forest. One of his roles in the forest is to trick us humans and, therefore, teach us tough lessons. He is not an evil being. But he is in the forest to defend its territory. Therefore, don't play with him having bad intentions. Ask him for something that you and your community need, and he will provide it to you."

Maryano Maya explained that to be a forest scholar means to be open to the unexpected. It also means learning from people who came before us, who explored African spirituality through patience and presence.

Maryano Maya's stories about the forest were fascinating, and before the forest scholars knew it, lunchtime arrived. Maryano Maya's family had prepared a homemade Brazilian dish called moqueca de camarão, a slowly cooked stew with fish, tomato, coriander, and onion, served in a clay pot. The forest scholars' mouths were watering as they enjoyed the meal, and Maryano Maya enthusiastically kept sharing more about the mystical lessons he learned from the forest.

Curious to know what lessons he shared with the scholars, young mystic? Here is a list:

LESSONS FROM THE FOREST

- The forest is here to teach you the ways of your ancestors.
- Be careful in the forest: Watch where you're walking, and be aware of falling branches from the older trees.
- Let someone know when you're going on a forest adventure, and use the buddy system.
- Nature teaches you to be gentle with yourself and to respect other beings.
- You are part of nature, just as important as the animals, plants, rocks, and sunshine.
- You can and should have sacred dialogues with the nature around and within you.
- Whenever you feel afraid, call on Saci, or your favorite spirit guides, to protect you.

Later that week, once back in the Bambo Forest, the scholars spent the morning outside in the garden, planting vegetable seeds. As he was covering some seeds with soil, Kossi looked up and noticed a tree that seemed to have an eye carved into it. Looking closer, he saw that the shape of the tree bark was what gave him the impression there was an eye.

Kossi decided to name this tree the Seeing Tree, because it was watching and studying him as he was watching and studying it. *We are nature observing itself*, Kossi recalled his dad telling him. *Everything we need to heal can be found in nature. Earth's natural medicine is often much closer to us than we think.*

FOREST FACTS ABOUT TREES

- Humans can be social when they want to be, and so can trees! Trees can count, learn, make decisions, and have memories (just like you!). They also have the power to heal other trees that are sick. Trees' ability to take care of one another is one of their most important spiritual lessons you're meant to learn.

• Spending time in nature, surrounded by trees, has been proven to decrease stress hormones in your body and boost your immune system's health throughout your life.

• Trees have memories, collective ones that they share with one another. They can also experience pain. Trees love living in communities and supporting one another.

• Trees and forests are encyclopedias of knowledge and natural pharmacies. Most medicine comes from trees, plants, and herbs.

How do you feel about trees, Forest Scholar? If you want, read this book (or any book) in a forest or near some trees. They'll be reading along with you, helping you remember.

Plants, like trees, hold incredible power and energy. Humans can benefit from many different plants for their well-being. Here are some key plants, flowers, and herbs used in Africa and around the world for their ability to heal and to make you healthier:

• **Ginger:** has so many benefits for your body! It gives you healthier skin, boosts your immune system so you can fight off viruses better, helps relieve the pain from an upset stomach, increases dopamine—known as the happy chemical—in your body, lowers blood sugar levels, and much more. Ginger is the most used plant in African spirituality.

• **Hibiscus:** this is a superfood that is high in vitamin C. It helps your body get rid of things that harm it. It also makes your heart work better and can help heal your skin. In Africa, it is often taken in juice form (which can be referred to as "bissap" in regions such as Togo, Bénin, and Côte d'Ivoire).

- **Chamomile:** helps prevent mosquito bites (which can protect people from malaria on the African continent in particular). It soothes itchy skin and helps reduce anxiety and tummy issues. It also helps you sleep better. Tea is a common form of taking in this flower.

- **Lavender:** has a calming effect on your body and mind. It helps with anxiety, stress, feeling nauseated, digesting foods better, soothing menstrual cramps, and sleeping well.

- **Rosemary:** good for boosting memory and your intellect. It can also boost your optimism and happiness. (Note: When planting rosemary, make sure it has plenty of sunshine, not too much soil, and a minimal amount of water.)

- **Turmeric:** is a healthy food with several benefits that's been used for over five thousand years. It comes from the same family as ginger, and it helps your body digest food better. You can also use it in a face mask to help your skin.

Bananas, almonds, peanuts, spinach, coriander, cacao, cashews, avocado, legumes, basil, sage, oregano, and spearmint have an important mineral called magnesium in them. Magnesium helps your body's bones, muscles, and nerves function properly. It helps you sleep better and boosts your energy levels.

While walking back to their cabins after Forest Magic School, the almost-twins stopped by the community garden to greet an elderly gardener named Chris, who was originally from the island of Jamaica.

"It took me years of study to become an expert herbalist and to recognize plants and memorize their properties," Chris shared as the almost-twins took in the beauty of all the plants around them. "Patience and presence are key to becoming deeply connected with nature, and with yourself, and others, too. There's a Forest Magic University here, where you can learn how to be an herbalist as you grow up."

As he said that, as if by magic, the university's head botanist, Professor Yapo, appeared from behind the *Mimosa pudica* plant, which is a plant that closes when it's touched. His co-professor, Diosa, was carrying a notepad and keeping track of their botanical journey.

While admiring the variety of vegetation in the garden, Yawa tripped and scratched her hand on a sharp rock. Her hand started bleeding. Tears rushed to her eyes, but she was present with the pain. She tried to breathe her way through it.

The gardener looked at her hand, then entered the garden's greenhouse with Professors Yapo and Diosa while Kossi stayed by Yawa's side. It was called the Ọsanyìn Greenhouse because it was named after the Òrìṣà of herbal medicine. This greenhouse was a healing pharmacy that housed hundreds of plants with their healing properties listed beside each.

The herbalists returned a few moments later. "This plant will stop the bleeding," explained Professor Yapo. "It's called the *Aspilia africana*. We use it as a natural first aid tool in the village when people get minor cuts such as this one." He grabbed the plant, wet it slightly with the help of the droplets of rain that were beginning to fall, and rubbed his hands together with it between his palms until the plant looked like a soggy spinach leaf. He laid the wet leaf on top of Yawa's wound, and within minutes, the bleeding stopped and the cut was beginning to heal. He then put the liquid found inside the *Aloe vera* plant on top of her wound as an extra layer of plant healing and natural protection.

"Magic!" Yawa and Kossi both said at the same time, as Yawa's hand was nursed back to health.

"*Plant magic,*" the gardener specified while smiling at the almost-twins, at himself, and at the nature around them.

On the fourth day of the sixth week, Yawa woke up earlier than usual and found that Kossi wasn't in his bedroom. She left Mami and Papi's house and eventually found her brother in the forest near a tree. Apparently, Kossi had been waking up early each morning to meditate and ground himself with his favorite tree. When Yawa found him, he had tears in his eyes, which he told her was because he felt so connected to the tree's roots.

Kossi's dad had always reminded him of the power of tears as a form of cleansing and release. And just that morning, Kossi had fallen while running toward his favorite tree to meditate, hurting his ankle. *Tears are transformational and an inherent part of who we are*, Kossi had quietly told himself as he lay on the ground and nursed his throbbing ankle. *I will breathe into my pain, using the* **Tonglen meditation** *method, and I will send love to my pain, without wishing it will immediately go away.*

What is the pain teaching me? Kossi had asked himself at the time. And that was when, as if by magic, Yawa had found him. She sat next to him, meditated silently for a minute, put her hand on his throbbing ankle, and breathed into the pain along with him.

The Cycles of Grief

While week six was in session, the almost-twins arrived at the Bamboo Room one day and noticed that their tablemate, Clémentine, wasn't there.

"Where's Clémentine?" they asked Professor Ori.

Professor Ori took a deep breath and asked the scholars to gather into the learning circle.

"Clémentine's mother transitioned last night," Professor Ori explained. "She's off to the world of the ancestors. Clémentine is grieving with her family."

"Transitioned?" Kossi asked.

"It means she passed away. Some people refer to this as death, but for many of us, we feel that Clémentine's mom isn't fully dead. Her energy has transformed from the physical form, but spiritually she is still with us."

"What are you talking about Professor Ori? What you are saying isn't true. Clémentine's mom is dead!" Kossi shouted as he ran out of the class.

Yawa got up to follow her brother, but Professor Ori calmly told her, "Yawa, Kossi needs some space. He's grieving. We all are. Let's take a moment to be with our grief and send our love to Clémentine's mom together."

After a brief silence, the forest scholars were introduced to the school therapist, Gueston, who entered the cabin classroom with

Kossi beside him. After a clockwork breathwork exercise, Gueston let the scholars know they were not alone in feeling **grief**.

"When I was fourteen, my younger sister passed away unexpectedly. At first, I refused to believe what happened. Later, I felt anger. There were times when I wished I could have been the one who had passed. The process of grieving is deeply confusing. I felt a rush of emotions. Deep sadness was one of my most present feelings, especially once I accepted what had happened."

The forest scholars held one another's hands as they reflected on what Gueston had just shared about grief.

"How did you keep going on?" Kossi asked after wiping away his tears. He couldn't even imagine Yawa not being in his life.

"I spent a lot of time in nature, and I found ways to let the grief move through me, rather than letting it be stuck in my body. I did sports. I screamed when I wanted to. I wrote in my journal a lot. I cried often. I learned to trust what I was feeling. Anyone who has dealt with the physical loss of someone they love knows that there's nothing anyone can really say to ease the feeling. The best way to help someone is to be present. Let them know you're there for them and that the person that transitioned is still with them. They just need to look for signs."

As soon as Gueston uttered those words, a swarm of bats flew outside the classroom, which they could see through the glass window of the Bamboo Room.

"Bats!" Kossi exclaimed in awe. "Papi always told me that bats represent our ancestors. Seems like Clémentine's mom is sending us a sign."

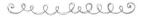

In African spirituality, ancestors' lives are celebrated after they physically leave the community. Their transition indicates that you now have another being in the ancestor realm watching over you. So that

Sunday, at Clémentine's mom's transition ceremony, many of the villagers were wearing the same fabric made in her favorite color orange and covered in **adinkra symbols**. The people gathered to celebrate the life and new beginning of their ancestor with dancing, crying, singing, drumming, praying, and eating. They sent prayers of protection to Oyá, the Òrìṣà of the cemetery and grief. The forest scholars and their families surrounded Clémentine and left her family dozens of offerings of fruit, vegetables, flowers, and plants. They honored and celebrated the life of Naëlle, Clémentine's mother.

After the memorial, Gueston gathered the forest scholars in a circle, surrounding Clémentine with their love, and shared a final thought with them before they left.

"Nature teaches us the cycles of life," he began. "We live. We grow. We are transformed. Look at the plants that grow from the ground. They all start small. Some grow to be huge trees, and some only grow to be small flowers. Some live for hundreds of years. Some live for only a few days before they go back to nourish the ground they came from."

As Gueston said this, he laid a bouquet of sunflowers near Clémentine's mom's memorial. "In the forest, where all is connected, the loss of one thing provides a passage for the life of another. In nature, death is a key part of the cycle of life. Plants die, rot, and give back nutrients to the soil. Animals die, and their bodies become food for other creatures.

"The forest also teaches us that grief is a natural part of life and that it is okay to experience it," Gueston continued. "Fallen trees and decaying leaves create nutrient-rich soil that supports new growth. In the same way, we can honor our loved ones by cherishing their memory and use what we've learned from them to support our own growth."

Growth Work

Think of the people, situations, plants, or animals in your life that you've had to say good-bye to. Maybe they didn't physically die, but maybe you used to be close to them and now they're no longer in your life. How did you work through the waves of grief that you felt during that experience?

Write a poem or song to help someone like Clémentine work their way through grief, using your own experiences or views on grief as inspiration. Remember, scholar: There's no wrong or right way to grieve. And grief may come in waves.

CHAPTER 7

As You Speak, You Create

Having gratitude—being thankful—will bring you even greater blessings and protection," Mami told the almost-twins at breakfast as they were getting ready to begin week seven of Forest Magic School. This morning they were eating boiled plantain and avocado toast, made with ripe avocados from Mami and Papi's tree. "I'm so grateful we've been able to be together these past two months, my loves. Life feels better when we're together."

"Àṣẹ!" Kossi and Yawa responded in unison. The expression Àṣẹ (pronounced ah-sheh) is a Yorùbá phrase meaning *having the power to make something happen*. It's like the phrase *and so it is*. It can also be a spiritual affirmation similar to *amen* for the Yorùbá people.

Àṣẹ also represents the inner energy, or life force, that exists in all beings.

Kossi and Yawa's parents often told them that the words *akpé kaka* (thank you very much in Mina) were like a lucky charm that increased their luck and brought more blessings into their lives. And through the time they had spent with their grandparents, the almost-twins saw that this was true. The more gratitude and thankfulness they showed for all they were learning and experiencing, the more blessings and opportunities to learn were sent their way by the universe. *What do you feel grateful for, Forest Scholar? Write a list in your journal of everything you're currently grateful for, and add to it whenever more comes to mind.*

On the first day of the seventh week of Forest Magic School, Yawa went for an early-morning walk, ending up at the Tawe Tree of Time, where she stopped to eat the mango she had brought with her. Yawa sat on the tree's roots, leafing through a book she had found in Mami and Papi's bookcase. The book was filled with African **proverbs**, written in different languages.

Yawa didn't yet know how to speak her indigenous languages fluently. She felt sad. "Why are you crying?" Yawa could feel the Tawe Tree asking her. "Don't get me wrong, my tree trunk enjoys the droplets of water, but I want to make sure you're okay."

"I . . . I want to feel more connected to my ancestry, but I am still learning Ewe, and Fon, and Yorùbá, and Baoulé. For now, I speak only English and French fluently."

"Language learning is like forest school learning. It happens day by day," the Tawe Tree whispered to her through the ruffles of leaves. "*Patience and presence.* Proverbs can recall memory and honor our ancestors in direct ways that are beyond simple language. Just as you have ancestral intelligence in your Ori, the proverbs that have been passed down from generation to generation also are learnings that guide and support you through life."

"By saying ancient proverbs, I'll connect to my African roots even more?" Yawa asked.

The Tawe Tree's branches shook yes softly.

Yawa was the first to arrive at the Bamboo Room, and Professor Ori, who spoke several indigenous African languages, could tell she was deeply interested in the proverb book.

"We can read them together, if you'd like," the professor told Yawa. "I'll recite them. And you repeat them." With each proverb Yawa and the professor recited, a forest scholar arrived in the room, joined them in the learning circle, and repeated the proverb, too. This was their collective learning.

Would you like to join the forest scholars and remember ancient proverbs, too?

Indigenous Proverbs from West Africa

· ·

EWE PROVERBS

Ðeviwo fe dumɛ didi n'tɔ.
"Dévio me doumé dʒi dʒi n'to."

Translation: The land of the children is very, very far away.

Meaning: This proverb shares the power and magic that exists in children. In Ɛwe culture, children are viewed as the closest connection the community has to God—or source. This proverb is a form of protection for kids and their childhood.

Ɛdu gbãgban, ɖeviwo fe nume wò senele.
"Ɛdougban gban dévio me nu ossénélé."

Translation: We first hear news of a village's destruction through the mouths of children.

Meaning: This proverb highlights the natural intelligence, psychic, and prophetic nature of children like you. To be prophetic means to see into the future. This proverb reminds you that children can often tell when an event is about to happen, and so their instincts should be trusted.

Adoglo be, wo nɛ biã gbe ɖeviwo ne wolɔ̃ madu fia.
"Adon'glo bé oné bio gbé dévio no'olon yéla doufio faa."

Translation: Let us ask the children; they will tell us who should or should not be king.

Meaning: This powerful proverb reminds the community to let children have their say when making community decisions. Children can and should be able to give their opinion and advice on community matters.

Ðevi ke nya asi asiklɔ ate ŋu aɖu nu kple fiawo.
"Devi deyna assikloklo éyé dounanou klé fiao."

Translation: A child who knows how to properly wash their hands will dine with royalty.

Meaning: As in all societies, certain customs in West Africa can help children evolve and grow. This proverb encourages young people to learn the way of the land and to be aware of traditional customs. This will help them attract amazing opportunities.

IGBO PROVERB

"Ɛjiro anya eji-afu mmada afu Mmuo."

Translation: The eye used in seeing human beings is not the eye used in seeing spirit.

Meaning: The spiritual world has plenty of things we do not see with our eyes but that we can feel with our souls.

YORÙBÁ PROVERB

"Odó t'ó bà gbùgbé orísun è, á gbẹ."

Translation: A river that forgets its source is bound to dry up.

Meaning: Always remember where you came from, and return to your roots regularly to honor yourself and your ancestry.

The sounds of the indigenous phrases felt like a calming trance. Yawa felt much better surrounded by her forest friends, who were open to learning and remembering along with her. Once the scholars were done reciting the proverbs, Professor Ori played them a guided-meditation audio recording from a spiritual empress (a woman who represents health, love, and wealth) who went by the name of La Sirène.

"You have just tapped into ancestral wisdom through the power of words, young mystics," La Sirène began in the meditation. "Your words have the power to create your reality. There's a reason that during the enslavement trade, those who oppressed the enslaved didn't want them to know how to read or write (but hundreds of thousands of enslaved Africans secretly learned or taught themselves how to do so anyway). Words have power. That's why Africa is the continent with the deepest oral tradition. That tradition can be kept alive in you by creating mantras and sharing affirmations that make your Ori feel great. Let's fill our Oris with uplifting mantras and choose to speak into existence what we would like to see happen, rather than living in fear of the worst that could happen. The universe is listening to you and the way we speak and think about yourself. So if you speak life into yourself by saying joyful and empowering phrases to your Ori, your life will gradually (and sometimes suddenly!) become a reflection of the words you speak."

MANTRAS YOU CAN SAY TO KEEP YOUR SPIRIT STRONG

- I am aware and present. I am protected.
- Create. Believe. Receive.
- I am a flower that helps other flowers open.
- Thank you, trees and plants and leaves. Thank you, seeds and ants and weeds. Thank you, sun, soil, soul, and sweat. Thank you, east, south, north, and west.
- I view the world as my home. That means I must respect the world as my home. I respect myself as my home.
- I am healthy, I am wealthy, I am safe, I am blessed!

In your journal, you can create your own mantras. They are most effective when you repeat them regularly, particularly when you're in a good mood and you feel connected to what you're saying.

The Power of Words

Your words have much more power than you could imagine. In African spirituality, words offer protection. So if you are feeling unwell, you wouldn't say, "I'm sick," but rather, "I am healing myself." In West African spirituality, sickness is not only when you are feeling bad in your body; it can also mean that something is unwell spiritually. Your Ori is alerting you to something. Ask your ancestors or family for support to help you feel better.

Saying "I'm sorry" when you hurt someone and asking for forgiveness from your ancestors, and from yourself, are essential parts of African spirituality. Yawa and Kossi had been taught to do so since a young age, so it was not uncommon to overhear the almost-twins tell each other, "I'm sorry I lost my patience with you," and "I apologize for raising my voice," and "I forgive you."

You also can find power in saying these words: "I forgive myself."

The Òrìṣàs want you to keep in mind that our ancestors want us to be responsible for the actions we take, the words we say, and the reactions we have.

The Power of Symbols

As the seventh week went by, the forest scholars and their professors went on a field trip to Ghana, the neighboring country of Côte d'Ivoire. Akua is from Ghana, and she was thrilled to show a part of her home to her forest friends. Ghana and Côte d'Ivoire used to be part of the same region before colonization, so there are more similarities between the two countries than there are differences. While in Ghana, they met local artists who helped the scholars create pottery engraved with adinkra symbols.

Adinkra symbols come from the area of Ghana and Côte d'Ivoire that used to be called the Kingdom of Ashanti. These symbols are ways that people connect spoken elements with ones you can see. These symbols also represent proverbs or spiritual concepts. The Asante people of Ghana and the Akan people of Côte d'Ivoire use adinkra symbols to decorate pottery and fabrics.

Yawa looked down at her favorite brass ring, which her mother had given her on her tenth birthday. There, on the ring, was the adinkra symbol sankofa, meaning *go back and get it*. It was a reminder to learn from your past. The Akan proverb it represented— se wo were fi na wosan kofa a yenkyiri—translated to *it is not taboo to go back for what you forgot (or left behind)*. Yawa thought about her journey of remembrance.

You're on this journey, too, young mystic. In your special journal, write down what you've been enjoying most from this exploration of African spirituality.

Maybe one of the adinkra symbols will help inspire you, and you can look them up and draw your favorite one in your journal and write down its meaning.

There are 122 adinkra symbols, each with its own special meaning, drawing, proverb, and protection. The forest scholars used nine of their favorites when creating their pottery. These nine symbols were:

- Mmere dane, meaning, *Time changes*
- Nea onnim no sua a ohu, meaning, *He who does not know can know from learning*
- Nsoromma, meaning, *Child of the heavens*
- Osram ne nsromma, meaning, *The moon and the star*
- Owo foro adobe, meaning, *The snake climbing the raffia tree*
- Sesa wo suban, meaning, *I change or transform my life*
- Akoma, meaning, *The heart*
- Akoma ntoso, meaning, *Linked hearts*
- Ananse ntontan, meaning, *Spider's web*

Animals as Symbols

Kossi and Yawa loved riding bikes through the forest, where they observed some of the animals there. A while ago, Mami and Papi explained to the almost-twins that each animal has a spiritual symbolism and that our spirits are sometimes drawn to certain animals over others. These animals—"spirit symbols"—can act as guides for you and to help you understand the world.

The almost-twins saw many spirit symbols in the forest, including:

A snake

The snake can be a symbol of kundalini energy, which is a dimension of energy that has yet to be awakened. Children who live joyful and protected lives tend to already have their kundalini energy awakened. Your role as a forest scholar is to keep that energy awake.

Snakes are honored in the West African country of Bénin. The python gives protective energy and can be a good sign. Snakes leave behind their skin, which reminds you of rebirth. A snake can appear on your path as a symbol that it's time to transform yourself.

Spiders

In the Akan tales, the spider Ananse (sometimes called Anansi) was viewed as the god of tricks, playfulness, wisdom, philosophy, storytelling, and knowledge. In several African societies, spiders are viewed as a good omen or a visit from the ancestors.

Monkeys

There are several monkeys in the Bambo Forest, as well as in countless African forests. Monkeys remind you to let yourself have more fun, while also remembering the value of community. Monkeys are also viewed as guardians of African tradition, including storytelling and rituals. Gift them bananas as offerings!

Peacocks

In Yorùbá spirituality, peacocks are viewed as sacred messengers between Africans and the creator, Olódùmarè. Seeing a peacock in a forest, or anywhere you are, is a good omen and a sign of luck, wisdom, protection, confidence, renewal, and immortality.

Dream Symbolism

In African spirituality, your dreams are a portal to another world, and that world gives you information about your waking life. They're viewed as the bridge between the ancestral world and the human world. They're the ancestors' main way of communicating with us. Paying attention to your dreams, and training yourself to remember your dreams, helps you activate your melanin magic.

TIPS FOR REMEMBERING YOUR DREAMS

• Make a drink out of the kinkéliba plant, and drink it each day.

- Keep a dream journal near your bed, or record a voice note each morning.
- Choose a variety of seven soaps, ideally each with a slightly different color. Add a mild amount of chopped ginger to the soaps, and pound them all together in a mortar until a new soap is created. Use that soap daily, and you'll notice that over time, it becomes easier to remember your dreams.

COMMON SYMBOLS IN AFRICAN DREAMS

- **Direct messages from ancestors:** seeing someone who has previously transitioned in a dream is a signal that they are still with you, protecting you, or maybe they're alerting you to something happening in your waking life that you should pay attention to.
- **Falling dream:** this may be a sign from ancestors that you're trying to control a situation too much, when instead you should leave them offerings and ask for their guidance and support. Allow yourself to be taken care of and held by your spirit guides.
- **Being chased in a dream:** having this dream several times in a row may mean your ancestors want you to look at your environment and whom you keep around you. Can they be trusted, or does your Ori feel strange or cautious around them? If there are new people you've recently let into your life, take time getting to know them.
- **Snake in a dream:** this is a sign that one phase of your life is ending and you may be changing or going through a cycle of rebirth.
- **Water in a dream:** you are being asked to either purify yourself (getting rid of old energy that no longer feels right for you) or to get more curious about your emotions and what they're trying to help you see. Calling on water deities such as Ọṣun and Oyá may help for dreams like this.
- **Friends repeatedly showing up in a dream:** pay attention to how your dream self feels around that friend in the dream. It is often a direct communication from your ancestors, letting you know your

friend's true intention. For example, if you repeatedly have a dream where a friend is talking about you behind your back, there is a strong likelihood that a part of you doesn't fully trust that friend in your waking life, and your ancestors may want you to distance yourself while you sort out the situation. If a friend you haven't talked to in a while shows up in your dream and you have a pleasant experience together, it may be a sign that your Ori wants you to reach out to that friend or maybe that friend will reach out to you soon.

The Power of Cowries

After dinner that day, the almost-twins and their grandparents sat out on the balcony surrounded by a canopy of palm trees. The forest monkeys came out to keep them company.

"Mami, did you know that cowries used to be a form of money?" Yawa inquired as Mami placed her hair into her favorite hairstyle—two afro puffs. Yawa had picked up a new book all about cowries at the Forest Magic School library. A cowrie is a sea snail whose shell has a glossy exterior. Yawa was fascinated by cowrie shells.

"Yes, they were used as currency throughout West Africa, as well as a form of trade. My grandmother often told me this, and she showed me her collection of cowries."

"Really? Do you still have the cowries?" Yawa asked.

Mami smiled as she finished doing Yawa's hair. "Come see. Kossi, Papi, you too."

The almost-twins and Papi followed Mami down a corridor, out into the garden, and up a wooden ramp into a tree house. She turned on the lights. A large magic chest decorated with cowrie shells along with a yellow rug was the only thing present in the room. Mami handed Yawa a golden key. Yawa unlocked the chest, and her eyes widened.

Her great-great-grandmother's collection of cowries, plus many of the goods she had earned during her time as a market woman, lay there in front of Yawa. Touching them felt like being transported back to that time long ago.

"Grandma Vovo was one of the best entrepreneurs of the forest village," Mami shared with pride. "Her Òrìsà was Yemọja, the goddess of the seas, represented by the cowries. Just like yours."

Yawa's eyes twinkled with happiness at this connection. She reminded herself to add cowries to her altar in her room, next to Grandma Vovo's portrait.

"What's an entrepreneur?" Kossi asked.

"An entrepreneur is someone who takes opportunities into their own hands, usually through creating a business or service, even if it means risking money. Africans are the original entrepreneurs."

"Especially African women," Papi added as he sat on the yellow rug. "Just look at how skilled many of the market women today are. Do you see how they gracefully carry several pounds of produce or gallons of water on their heads daily? How they're able to withstand the sun's blistering heat and show up for their community and families each day? There's a reason we call this continent Mother Africa. But that's also why we should honor, protect, and take care of Mother Africa, and all living beings. We can't expect others to be of service to us, or for the earth to keep taking care of us. We must pour into Mother Nature, and she will then pour into us. Imagine pouring water onto a potted plant, as an offering to Mother Nature, and the water overflowing from the pot and going back into the earth. That's a form of reciprocity—a mutual exchange of energy. Cowries were used by our ancestors to thank entrepreneurs for the services and goods they provided."

Yawa found her great-great-grandmother's notebook in the cowrie chest. It was filled with research notes and facts about cowries and their spiritual origins. Reading it, the almost-twins learned that cowries were placed in Kemet on top of mummies to represent their vision in the afterlife. Both the Kemites and the Yorùbá people viewed cowrie shells as gifts from deities.

The cowrie resembles both an eye and a mouth, encouraging you to be authentic and true to what you have to say and to what you see. It can also be viewed as a seed, so during new moon passages (when the moon is not visible in the sky, or when the first crescent appears in the sky), writing your intentions with a cowrie shell nearby, or placing a cowrie shell on your altar, can bring you extra protection.

"Yemọja is represented by the cowries because she's viewed as the mother of all," Mami reminded the almost-twins. "And since all of humankind originated in Africa, all humans benefit from honoring Yemọja. Our ancestors believed that when they treated the ocean and other bodies of water with respect, Yemọja was pleased and would ask the ocean to leave cowrie shells on the shore as a gift to the world. This was viewed as a blessing from Yemọja, and that's part of the reason cowries became a type of money."

Mami handed the almost-twins the glossy shells, and they observed the shells' narrow openings.

"Cowries weren't only viewed as money," Papi said as the family headed back to get ready for bed. "They are also viewed as a way to send positive energy and luck. The Yorùbá use them for divination to help look into the future, the past, the present, and the world beyond all time. We call this the spirit world."

"How could the cowrie shells show what was going to happen in the spirit world?" asked Yawa once they were in the cabin house.

"Each arrangement of cowries tells a specific story."

"And how can we tell what that story is?" Kossi asked.

Papi could tell that his grandkids were still curious, so when he tucked them into bed, he pulled out his favorite book on Obi divination and read them a few parts. The almost-twins learned that cowries could be used as "portals of spiritual communication," meaning that with patience and presence, they could be used to talk to spirits.

Yawa stayed up later than usual and used her SpacePad to do more research. She found out that there were different forms of cowrie divination, but that Obi divination was the most commonly practiced by the Yorùbá. Obi divination is traditionally done using a kola nut, but people of the diaspora and of the continent also use cowrie shells today. Yawa continued reading and found out more information about how to divine using cowries:

• For beginners, four shells are typically used when divining.

• It's best to stick with yes/no questions when divining with cowrie shells.

• There are multiple outcomes for how the four shells can fall. After being thrown, the shells either land open or closed. This is what the different outcomes mean:

  – **Oyekun:** four mouth-down cowries. This represents a very firm no. When all the cowrie shells face down, the spirits of your ancestors are speaking clearly, and you must listen.

  – **Alafia (peace):** four mouth-up cowries. This symbolizes a yes to whatever you asked about. It's a sign that the doors are open. You may have to ask more questions for greater detail on what your next step should be.

  – **Okanran:** one mouth-up, three mouth-down cowries. This represents a no. The expression translates to: "three have teamed up against one." The ancestors have closed the door, most likely for your protection. It's best to ask another question to get more information on what the no is for, or how to turn it into a yes.

- **Etawa (maybe):** three mouth-up, one mouth-down cowries. This represents that the answer isn't sure. The word etawa means "one has turned against three others." You can think of this as a meeting in the village. If not everyone at the meeting agrees on a point, then they need to deliberate more. To deliberate means careful thought about next steps, and that's what this cowrie divination outcome represents. You should ask another question to get a clearer answer.

- **Ejife (a clear yes):** two mouth-up and two mouth-down: this outcome signifies a clear yes from the ancestors. You can trust that what you're asking for is spiritually approved.

Obi divination with cowries can help you answer questions or know what you should do in the future. The energy of the cowries connects you to your ancestors and to the cosmos. The cowries help you feel seen, supported, loved, and protected. Remember that it's best to do cowrie divination with someone who is initiated in this spiritual practice, meaning they've undergone the necessary training to provide you with accurate results.

Growth Work

Do you know where you can find cowrie shells where you live, Forest Scholar? Ask a trusted adult to help you find an African market nearby, or an indigenous boutique shop. If you do find cowries, or if you or someone you know has some, add these magical shells to your collection of spiritual tools, and use them in whatever way makes you feel happy. Cowries are a direct connection to earth, and a reminder that there are many ways to be and feel rich.

CHAPTER 8
Eight Means Infinity

T he Forest Magic School Fair took place during the eighth week. It always took place outside in the market as a way for the forest scholars and their families to tap into the natural abundance of earth. The community exchanged different goods with one another, and not necessarily by using money. For example, if a bread-maker wanted a pot of honey and a honey-maker wanted sweet bread, the two forest friends could exchange products and both be satisfied. This form of nonmonetary exchange is called bartering. Yawa and Kossi loved watching these interactions because it made them feel connected to the supportive Bambo community.

"*Abundance is everywhere*," Ascension Adam had shared with the scholars via an email they had received in their SpacePads. "My forest friend Adela often reminds me that scarcity is a human-made invention. Look at the abundance of trees, leaves, birds, clouds, air, and life around you right now. And most important, look at your health. You're alive, you're breathing, you're growing. To most Africans, great health is the ultimate sign of wealth, including the wealth of the children, whether they are your own children or the children of the village. Children represent wealth."

Music as Ancestral Offerings

Remember those drums that Yawa and Kossi heard in the distance as they walked through the forest on their first day in the village? In West African spirituality, drums are one of the most direct ways to connect with one's ancestors and to welcome their energy into the world today. Many West African drummers (and musicians) play with intent, or purpose, because it connects them to another world that cannot necessarily be seen but that is felt. African musical instruments are like a bridge to communicate with the human spirit and the cosmic spirit. Today, many of these instruments are still made using ancient crafting techniques and natural materials. The most commonly played instruments in Africa are the drums, rattles, shakers, and the xylophone, though part of the magic of African music is the power to create music with whatever is around you, like pots, pans, spoons, baobab fruits, your hands, your voice, snapping fingers, and anything your Ori can imagine.

Midweek, at the bonfire, the forest scholars and their family took part in a live musical performance. Yawa grabbed the mbira, an instrument native to Zimbabwe and made from a wooden board attached to metal tines. It gave off a chime-like sound. Kossi grabbed some clappers, which are a basic percussion instrument made by striking two objects together. (Clappers are one of the most ancient instruments in Africa, commonly used by the Kemites during celebrations, funerals, and rituals.)

Ife and Clémentine came through with bell instruments such as the gankogui, which came from the Ewe tribe and is a double bell made from forged iron. A wooden stick is used to strike against the bell and make a powerfully deep sound. Sundiata took the shells of two dried coconuts and used them as her instrument of choice. Michael pulled out his collection of cowries and began shaking them. Akua and Felipe started harmonizing with their voices.

Papi grabbed his favorite instrument, the kora, from Mali. When he started playing it, everyone took a deep breath. The kora, a stringed instrument with twenty-one strings (ten played with one's right hand and eleven with one's left), is known to have one of the most soothing effects on the human spirit. Mami played her flute, which she made by hand long ago using the wood from fallen branches.

The leaves of the trees swished, adding more rhythm to the collective vibrations. The birds sang along, too. The bonfire ceased once Ṣàngó and Oyá's lightning bolts began to appear, showing that the musical messages were heard and welcomed.

Forest Magic School Playlist

CHECK OUT THESE ARTISTS FROM AFRICA AND ITS DIASPORA!

Ali Farka Touré, Toumani Diabaté, Sona Jobarteh, Steven Amoikon, Magic System, Jidenna, Wizkid, Rema, Burna Boy, Célia Cruz, Les Garagistes, Master KG, Hope Masike, Salif Keita, Pierrette Adams, Dossé-Via, Bob Marley

*Which of your favorite musicians would
you add to your playlist?*

Auras as Protection

When the almost-twins woke from their afternoon nap, their bodies felt amazing. And not only did their personal energies seem to vibrate better, but the overall energy and aura of the forest around them did, too.

 An aura is an energy field that surrounds the physical body. It's often associated with a distinct color.

Here's how to tap into your aura energy:

• Pay attention to your auric field, which is the energy surrounding your body. Think, *Whom and what do I keep around me, and why?*

• Pay attention to whom you are around. Does your energy feel good around a certain person? Do you feel like you are losing energy around someone else? This can also be true for the TV shows you watch, the music you listen to, the books you read, the people you talk to (note that gossiping sucks away energy), and the food you eat.

It's essential to learn how to protect yourself and your aura. You can do so by following this advice:

• Try not to answer every call, email, text message, or request to speak in person you receive. Give yourself time to respond. Release the sense of urgency you or society might place on yourself. Understand the power of saying no and letting your energy guide you.

• Use plant medicine to make protective baths, soaps, or perfumes to ward off unwanted energy (only do this with the help of an herbalist and with your guardians' permission).

• Get at least eight hours of sleep a day, but also include moments of consistent physical activity in your day. Try not to use technology right before going to sleep or right after waking up. Instead, breathe, hydrate, and stretch so your energy and aura can be strong and you'll feel revitalized, meaning you'll experience a boost in energy.

The Protection of Resting Your Body

For the rest of the eighth week of Forest Magic School, the young scholars had only one mission assigned to them: rest.

Be like a tree and rest. Kossi remembered what Tata Soleil had taught them in Forest Magic School's science class: If you look up an image of the human body's nervous system and the root system of a tree, you'll notice that they're strikingly similar.

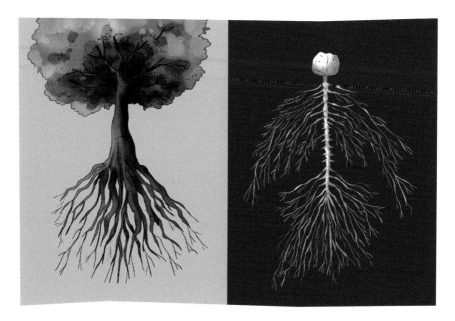

By now, the forest scholars had practiced clockwork breathwork regularly enough that it had become a habit. Being aware of their breath, their posture, and their energy helped them feel and live better. They breathed easier. Their Oris tingled more. And they enjoyed naps after lunch every day.

Professor Infinity wanted the scholars' minds to be still, so all SpacePads were shut down. No need to research, examine, debate, or ask questions. Just time to simply rest.

"Our ancestors did more than just work," Professor Infinity said. "They practiced rest and relaxation as a way of life. They were crafty with the work they did. They worked together, so they used their time better, allowing them to work smarter, not harder. This is the danger of societies that get too focused on being an individual rather than a community. It takes a village for everyone to be able to rest. A village that leans toward peace."

Forest Magic School feels like a peaceful village, Kossi thought to himself as he yawned and lay down in his hammock.

Cosmic Considerations

Most manifestation happens in our sleeping state, which is another world of its own that we have the power and wisdom to tap into, remember, and be fully present with.

We aren't yet sure which state of consciousness is "real": our sleeping/dreaming world or our waking one.

Village Rituals for Young Mystics

• Each African village has its own customs, and one of them has to do with protection rituals to keep their children safe. This could be doing a protective bath with healing plants, praying over children, or having them wear a spiritually protective piece of jewelry. It takes patience and presence to learn these rituals, and they are often passed down orally from generation to generation.

• When we eat, we should thank the animals, the plants, the water for their sustenance—their ability to provide us with energy, which then allows us to pour into Mama Earth and feel protected by her.

• Dancing is a big part of African spirituality, especially in the village, and children get to learn the magic of drumming at a young age. It activates their spirit. In African spirituality, drums are the instrument that connects us most directly with the ancestors. A portal to and from the ancestral world. An invitation for our ancestors to be present with us.

Growth Work

You, too, young learners immersed in this world, you must make time to rest. You should do so now when you are young and when you're older. Rest is healthy for the mind, body, and soul. Even if there's something on your to-do list, choosing to rest instead feels nice. Do that more often, and see how it makes you feel.

CHAPTER 9

Ascend and Expand

By the time the last week of Forest Magic School arrived, the forest scholars found their connection to one another stronger than ever. They gathered in the Bamboo Room the day before graduation and were each given an Akan hat to decorate for the ceremony. They also received copper chains with the symbol of an **ankh** on them.

As they excitedly decorated their Akan hats, the forest scholars heard the sound of drums playing in the forest. The wind was blowing a soft breeze through the windows. They slowly sipped water from a glass to stay hydrated. And candles were lit to inspire presence and creative inspiration. All

the elements were with them, celebrating all they had learned in the past two months.

Finally, the big moment had arrived. The forest scholars had completed their rite of passage through a successful and memorable nine-week journey at Forest Magic School, learning the ways of their ancestors. On graduation day, once everyone was settled in the forest auditorium, Professor Ori went onstage and said, "Today is not about us, scholars. You already know how proud we are of you. Today, on this final day of Forest Magic School, your Oris will do the talking. Remember those letters you wrote to your Ori on the first day here? If you feel the call, please pull out your papyrus journals and share a line or two with our community. Your Ori led you to this manifestation, scholars. Let your Oris speak."

One by one, the forest scholars went to the stage and let their Oris speak. They formed their learning circle, and then each scholar took a turn to enter the middle of the circle to share their message they had written to their Ori. Here is what they learned:

> *"Ori, the main thing I want to learn from Forest Magic School is how to breathe, just like the trees."*
> —Kossi

> *"Ori, when I look at my hands, I see my grandma's hands. Ori, help me feel even more connected to my grandma during my time at Forest Magic School. I miss her physical presence, and I want to feel her spiritually with me, guiding me."*
> —Akua

> *"Ori, remind me that I am the light peeking through the bamboo branches. The light I see is a reflection of the light that's within me."*
> —Sundiata

"Ori, the universe is always expanding, and so am I. Help me expand, grow, and breathe, like a plant, flower, or baby giraffe."
—Michael

"Ori, help me measure time by the number of conscious breaths I take."
—Ife

"Ori, we live in a world of infinite possibilities. Remind me of what it feels like to be infinity."—Clémentine

"Ori, there was once a world within a world, where all the worlds existed. That world is within you. That world is you."
—Felipe

"Ori, help me be present and patient with myself. Help me connect to my inner nature through being one with nature. Help me trust myself, others, the cosmos, and life itself."
—Yawa

Once all the scholars were seated in the learning circle, they held one another's hands and took a deep breath. On their first day, Professor Ori had told them that the forest would help them remember. And the forest world they had grown to cherish had, indeed, helped them remember so many truths about being connected to nature and the spiritual world.

"When we see you living your magically melanated life, connected to the power of the forest, to your ancestors, and to your breath, we feel even more connected to our own melanin magic and our inner child," Professor Ori said gratefully as they concluded their end-of-summer ceremony. "Thank you, Forest Scholars, for being present and patient. Thank you for trusting your Ori, knowing your roots, and letting yourself make mistakes. Thank you for bringing even more life to life."

The almost-twins were celebrating with Mami and Papi after graduation when they heard two familiar voices coming from behind the Seeing Tree. It was their parents, who had proudly witnessed the almost-twins' graduation ceremony. They were carrying big bouquets of flowers and a basket filled with their favorite fruit: mango.

The almost-twins and their parents hugged. All four of these beings' eyes filled with tears of joy. The mango tree's leaves quietly provided them with shade—it even seemed to be smiling back at them.

AFTERLUDE

Your journey exploring the forest, and African spirituality, is just beginning. It's a journey you will take your entire life, and one that takes patience and presence. The most important way to be on this journey is to be aware of the power of your Ori. This knowledge exists within you and is a part of you.

Below you'll find Growth Work to help you explore your melanin magic. The terms and concepts in the list below will help you further study African spirituality. Do this work at your own pace. Take it breath by breath and step by step.

- African numerology
- The ancient history of Sudan
- Bantu cosmology of Congo
- The benefits of shea butter and coconut oil
- California's name origin (most likely named after the Black queen Califia)
- Candomblé (Afro-Brazilian spirituality)
- Capoeira
- The Dogon and Sirius B
- The Great Pyramids of Giza
- Hieroglyphics
- Kemetic yoga poses (pose of Min and pose of Immortality)
- The meaning of the number nine in African spirituality
- The Mermaid Temple in Bénin
- Queen Nefertiti
- The Nubian Village
- The river that flows beneath the Nile
- Kwanzaa

What else would you like to learn about African spirituality, Forest Scholar? Be guided by your Ori.

SOURCES, RESOURCES, AND ADDITIONAL READING

Contributors

Adam Mota (Ascension Adam) motamanifest.com

Dossé-Via Trenou (the author) dossevia.com

Etche Innocents Tanyoeton (Professor Infinity)

Ethel-Ruth Tawe (The Tawe Tree of Time) artofetheltawe.com

Folu Oyefeso (culture journalist) foluoyefeso.com

Gueston Smith (Gueston the Grief Therapist) guesscreative.com

Maryano Maya from Brazil

Special thanks to botanist Mr. Yapo Nguessan, Michael N'Dah, and the forest of Banco community in Côte d'Ivoire

Websites for further SpacePad research

africa.si.edu

ancestralvoices.com

behealthyafrica.com

blackhistory.com

contemporary-african-art.com

knowthezodiac.com (calculate your birth chart for free)

originalbotanica.com

panaramiconline.com

yorubaizm.com

Books

The Hidden Life of Trees by Peter Wohlleben

Igbo Proverbs for Kids by Nna Nna and Nne Nne

Introduction to Igbo Mythology for Kids (Igbo Myths) by Chinelo Anyadiegwu

Knowing the Orisha Gods & Goddesses by Waldete Tristao

Yoruba Mythology Coloring Book: The Gods and Goddesses of Yorubaland by Nzinga-Christina Reid

GLOSSARY

Adinkra symbols: symbols from the area of Ghana and Côte d'Ivoire used as ways to connect spoken elements with ones you can see. These symbols also represent proverbs or spiritual concepts.

Ankh: a Kemetic symbol of life. It provides blessings, protection, good luck, and healing energy to those who wear it.

Bissap: a drink made of the hibiscus flower roselle.

Dashiki: a colorful item of clothing, often a shirt, that's quite common in West Africa.

Divination: a supernatural way of receiving knowledge about the future.

Grief: the deep sorrow that you feel when you say good-bye to something or someone that has died in either a physical or mental way.

Intergenerational learning: when communities of all ages teach one another and grow together equally.

Kente cloth: a handwoven textile from the region of West Africa now known as Ghana. It was first worn by royalty from the Akan tribe.

Luminary: a natural, light-giving body, in this case the sun and the moon.

Ori: our divine head and intuition.

Òrìṣàs: West African deities, supernatural forces of nature, native to the Yorùbá culture.

Proverb: a short statement that has a strong spiritual and practical meaning.

Rite of passage: a ceremony or event marking an important stage in one's life.

Solar new year: the start of a new twelve-month cycle that occurs from one birthday to the next.

Solar return: the moment the sun returns to the same position it was in when you were born.

Tonglen meditation: a Buddhist meditation that focuses on the "giving and receiving" energy present in breathwork.

Vitality: having strength and active energy.

ACKNOWLEDGMENTS

Writing this spirituality guide for young mystics was made possible thanks to my divine ancestors, my magical children, my curious inner child, and the Òrìṣàs.

Thank you to my phenomenal agent Meg Thompson, my brilliant editor Julie Matysik and the entire RP Kids team, and the talented illustrator Catmouse James for cocreating *Melanin Magic* with me and supporting my vision.

I'm infinitely grateful to my maternal and paternal grandparents for guiding me back to the motherland, and I give thanks to Mama Africa for being a constant source of wonder and inspiration for my children and me.

Thank you to *you*, young mystic, for trusting me as your guide through Forest Magic School. May the adventures continue.

ABOUT THE AUTHOR

DOSSÉ-VIA TRENOU is an author, artist, astrologer, and educator from West Africa. She is passionate about exploring the wonders and mysteries of African spirituality with her children, Nova Yawa and Rémy Kossi. Dossé-Via studied narrative studies at the University of Southern California and received her master's in English education from Teachers College, Columbia University. Dossé-Via is also the founder of the pan-African travel agency Magic & Melanin, which offers healing homegoing trips to people of the African diaspora. She envisions and creates a world where the depth of Africa's rich cultures and heritage is respected, shared, and credited, and where all the motherland's children feel proud of who they are, where they come from, and why they're here.